'This extraordinary piece of written art is an emotional rollercoaster of raw pain, humour and resilience. O'Reilly pushes the complexity of being human defined within a D/deaf and disabled context – a world which refutes and battles against ableist words of cure, to be fragmented, unfinished, damaged goods. Each monologue is whole and holistically rich and all resonate for the disabled and non-disabled reader. The poignant message is we are not ever going to disappear and we make no apology. This is a book for anyone who treasures the diversity of the world.'

Jenny Sealey – CEO/Artistic Director, Graeae Theatre

'I absolutely loved these plays…brilliant…profound…O'Reilly's collection of plays balances with expert precision both commonalities and particularities of disability experiences across many boundaries: international borders, identities, impairment types, languages, and cultures. Each play addresses the complexities of disability, Deaf, or illness experiences. Disability pride includes feelings of belonging but also deep ambivalence about the pain, suffering, oppression, and alienation those of with disabilities endure. The lyrical and collective voice of disability experience in these plays make me proud to be part of this remarkable community.'

Carrie Sandahl – Scholar, practitioner, activist

T0353542

the 'd' monologues

Kaite O'Reilly

THE 'd' MONOLOGUES

OBERON BOOKS
LONDON

WWW.OBERONBOOKS.COM

First published in 2018 by Oberon Books Ltd
521 Caledonian Road, London N7 9RH
Tel: +44 (0) 20 7607 3637 / Fax: +44 (0) 20 7607 3629
e-mail: info@oberonbooks.com
www.oberonbooks.com

PB ISBN: 9781786826350
E ISBN: 9781786826343

Cover image: Sophie Stone in *In Water I'm Weightless*
© FarrowsCreative

For all the glorious freaks of nature, the brittle-boned beauties,
the gems of the genome; the marvels, the rare jewels of genetic code,
dodo diamonds of DNA: You amaze me. I salute you.
I dedicate this to you all.

With thanks foremost to my community, one that is multiple and knows no borders or limitations. Thanks also to my collaborators, interviewees, supporters, funders, and all who made this collection possible.

Contents

Preface in Three Voices   1

Introduction   8

In Water I'm Weightless   11

richard iii redux
(co-written with Phillip Zarrilli)   75

And Suddenly I Disappear…
The Singapore/UK 'd' Monologues   133

Preface in Three Voices

In her glorious monologue *A Short History of Fear*, Kaite O'Reilly takes a litany of insults directed at disabled people: '*the mongs, the spazzies, the shunned, the feared*', and turns this list into a vision of greatness. It is a masterpiece of poetic and dramatic transformation. It is also a particularly resonant example of the juxtapositions of tone and language typical of O'Reilly's writing in general, and this volume in particular. Where else could you find a profound re-imagining of Shakespeare's *Richard III* weaving around nostalgia for the Bay City Rollers, or the lyrical inspiration of *Be a River* just around the corner from the vicious parody of *Non-Believer*. '*You have to be cruel to be kind. And I'll smash your fucking face in if you tell me otherwise*'.

The pieces in the volume have been performed in a variety of ways, but unlike much of O'Reilly's earlier work, they take the dramatic monologue as their organising principle. Gone here are the complex temporal and dramaturgical structures of earlier pieces such as *Perfect* and *Henhouse*, instead we have an exploration of the solo dramatic voice, the moment of acting and its confrontation with text. By boiling her theatre down to this simple question of the monologue, O'Reilly delivers perhaps her most thorough exploration to date of the nature of theatre – and of the ways in which the body of the disabled performer deconstructs and challenges our assumptions about stage and society. Certainly, *richard iii redux (OR Sara Beer Is/*

Not Richard III), which sits at the centre of the collection, is a mighty investigation of these questions. By introducing the actor who performs the monologue in the title of the work, O'Reilly/ Zarrilli instantly deconstruct the notion of performance, of representation, of the neutral body – '*I'm an actor about to play Richard the Third. Do you have any books on deformities?*' – reminding us instead that there is only ever specificity, difference, and that the dramatic text is always deeply implicated in the world that has produced it.

Around this central meditation on acting, other *'d' Monologues* circulate in this book, presented always as a range of possibilities, never as a prescriptive text. While *richard iii redux* can, in a way, never be properly performed by anyone other than Sara Beer, and can only be improperly performed by Beer herself as she fails brilliantly to become the Shakespearian anti-hero, the other *'d' Monologues* here are invitations to interpretation. They have been selected and structured in different ways by different performers, with a different shape and size each time. There is no normative 'd' monologue!

Indeed, as this collection of beautifully disparate works demonstrates, there is no normative O'Reilly, no one view, no single proposition about theatre or life, to recognise and write about, or enact. Rather this body of work is a disruptive flow, asking all of us to stop and make time for difference: to recognise the ever-unexpected emergence of the extraordinary.

John E McGrath
Artistic Director, Manchester International Festival

2.
'I'M SORRY. I'M SO, SO SORRY. IT WILL HAPPEN TO YOU.'

To recognise Disability Arts as a nuanced, distinct and powerful art genus always seems to be an uphill struggle. Non-disabled arts practitioners often view this solely from a community, marginalised or therapeutic model. Therefore, making connections into mainstream opportunities continues to be fraught with misunderstanding and barriers. Kaite O'Reilly is one of the few disability arts rooted artists to have made this impact. Kaite is a master in capturing atypical realities through beauty, challenge, connection and compassion. This is made clear through *The 'd' Monologues*, a plethora of gifts of insights into real disabled and Deaf lives, usually all too easily ignored within today's prevailing ableist society.

Her stories are vital as a voice from our disabled community and a tangible demonstration of how arts and disability expose the truth of the lived experience of disability. Kaite is hard hitting in her words whilst being humorous and engaging:

'I mean when people pass me on the street. There's a little click of the tongue and 'Bless. Love her...' There I am, exalted again.' (From *Walkie Talkies.*)

It is difficult to be critical or prejudiced when you are laughing along with a character's anecdotes. Kaite's versatility and placing of humour, poignancy and musing has the effect of endearing rather than dislocating or discomforting the viewer: the history and absurdity of *Richard III*, the contemporary setting of *In Water I am Weightless* with its immediate opening *'I'm so, so sorry. It will happen to you'* – illustrates that disability issues belong to us all. Kaite's work blatantly pushes through the 'them (disabled) and us (non-disabled)', capturing the belongingness and acceptance that we should all embrace.

Kaite's latest work – *And Suddenly I Disappear* – is a work designed to explore the culture context of disabled life in Singapore and the UK. Working with characters (and actors) from both countries, the piece depicts the commonalities of the disabled/Deaf person, and how they fit, or otherwise, into their own cultural contexts, demonstrating layers of complexities and misunderstandings. The impact of faith, and societal/family assumptions are disquietly exposed, each actor using a rich mix of stories through British and Singaporean perspectives.

Seizing upon scenes and events from the lived experience of disability, the harsh and honest truth of these reflections and observations hit home with immense passion, using the most perfect and beautiful wordcraftship. They also expose the cultural differences we face in each country. Disability is still a very contentious area for many places, and by creating cross-cultural work Kaite encourages an emergence of invisible hidden people. Therefore, I feel this work starts to take on a new urgency, so needed against austerity and the rise in international right wing politics. We have a window that is slowly opening and need to create work that will push this small opening wide.

In *The 'd' Monologues*, Kaite places the disabled voice centre stage, the solos and dialogues fashion conversations that create a catalyst for change or affirmation as a reflection of hidden realities. The very presence of disabled actors and their characters often creates the first challenge or even discomfort for punters, especially when equipped with powerful words, shedding insight and perspectives upon the many hidden and 'deliberately' forgotten stories. Thus, an exchange is applied as audiences are presented with perhaps awkward moments that can change their understanding of the truth of disability.

Without doubt, Kaite is one of the most important writers of her generation, creating poignant and relevant work, unflinching in confronting the impact of a disablist world, exposing the damage of a prevailing capitalist society and antagonising brunt austerity measures.

Ruth Gould MBE, DL
Artistic Director, DaDaFest

3.

'BE LIKE WATER. BE LIKE A RIVER...UNSTOPPABLE. FLUID. POWERFUL. MALLEABLE BUT INDEPENDENT, FOLLOWING YOUR OWN ROUTE, YOUR OWN WAY FROM SOURCE UNTIL YOU REACH AND MERGE WITH THE SEA.'

The task was not easy – create a work that resonates internationally, that drives forward change, that flexes and adapts to spaces and places, restrictions and opportunities, and do so on budget and on time. And of course, Kaite O'Reilly has done that – and done so brilliantly – with this collection of monologues and their frame. And to be honest, we'd expect nothing less.

Kaite's track record is strong, solid and sound – as she dances between form and content creating the most political of works reframing the experiences of disabled people and then to other work focusing just as powerfully on other issues. You might try, but you can't put her in a box.

Through *And Suddenly I Disappear,* Kaite un-boxes others. She has one ear for truth and another for justice, and within this work finds many compelling ways to make us listen. Based on testimony from disabled people both in Singapore and the UK, these tight and honed pieces simultaneously punch on both a personal and political level. Taking into account history, class, experience and the infinite variety of disabled people, the multiplicity of voices and perspectives we get to meet within this work is both how we see the world, and how we find a new and visible place within it.

The way Kaite takes language – multiple languages – and plays with it is masterful; everyone gets to experience just a taste of the isolation that one has when witnessing work performed in a different language, and then we are all whisked into a far greater joy and appreciation of the variety of ways in which we can express ourselves as no meaning is lost or unclear.

She also creates a new model – a piece that is a sum of its parts yet where all the parts themselves can change and interchange. In her own performances of the work, she uses technology to both aid access and to increase the representation within the room and supports emerging performers to find their voices and their spotlights. The impact of this work in Singapore cannot be overestimated, radically reimagining what is possible through direct action and address. As the piece moves forward to the UK, the addition of new monologues enable a local resonance that opens up the work to new audiences – an experience that can be repeated wherever the work is toured.

Kaite wanted to create a work that could have the same impact and future life as *The Vagina Monologues:* A work that could be reformed and restaged at multiple levels – from large scale performances to a group of disabled people in a rehearsal room text in hand – even one that offers pieces that disabled people might choose for the hardest of situations – auditions. And do you know what? I think with this work she might just have done that.

Jo Verrent
Producer, artist, activist

Introduction

I like to think of theatre as a place of communication and exploration, of dissent and inquiry: a place of dreaming, of solving, of challenging the present and imagining the future. It's that communal place where we can express all the possibilities of what it is to be human – so why are the majority of representations still so limited in scope and variety, and the potential of those bodies so prescribed?

I have been angry most of my life. Identifying as a working class Irish immigrant disabled female creates a certain kind of friction, a blistering energy I've found best directed into creative pursuits. Some years ago, somewhere along my raging, cursing way, I encountered Gandhi's advice about being the change you want to see, and so the project *The 'd' Monologues* was born.

These collected solos are the culmination of a decade's work trying to instigate change through writing work specifically for D/deaf and disabled actors, 'answering back' to the largely negative representations of difference in our media and the Western theatrical canon.

Since the Ancient Greeks disabled characters have appeared in plays, but rarely have the writers been disabled or written from that embodied or politicised perspective. The vast majority of disabled characters in the Western theatrical canon are tropes, reinforcing limited notions of what it is to be 'normal' rather than broadening the lens and embracing all the possibilities of human variety. So prevalent is the atypical body in our stage and TV dramas, the audience(s) assume they know and understand the realities of disabled and D/deaf individuals' lives, yet few of these narratives are informed by lived experience, and so misconceptions and ableist notions of difference, shaped by the medical and charity models of disability, are reproduced and reinforced.

I wanted to make work solely for disabled and D/deaf performers, informed by the social model of disability. Like gender, I believe that disability is a social construct, and it is the physical and attitudinal barriers which disable us, not the idiosyncrasies of our bodies.

This collection is the culmination of ten years' work, with fictional monologues inspired by over one hundred interviews, conversations, and interactions with D/deaf and disabled individuals internationally. It brings together new and previously unperformed texts alongside monologues from *In Water I'm Weightless* (National Theatre Wales/Cultural Olympiad 2012), the 70 minute one woman show *richard iii redux,* and the multilingual, intercultural *And Suddenly I Disappear.*

I've always loved the notion of disabled and D/deaf performers all over the world presenting with pride and political urgency performance texts which did not reduce them to parodies, metaphors, villains, or inspiration porn stars – different narratives using alternative dramaturgies, theatre languages and channels of communication. These texts did not exist, so following Gandhi's advice, I decided to be the change I wanted to see.

I began my explorations of the monologue in 2008 on a Creative Wales Major Award, courtesy of Arts Council Wales. As part of my development, I had interactions with world class exponents of the form including Eve Ensler, who immediately gave me vagina envy with her V Day. I've always dreamed of an international event challenging negative representations of difference and showcasing the very real talent which exists within our often over-looked communities. The monologue form is portable, flexible, and affordable to stage, either alone or in groups, script-in-hand with little rehearsal, or fully produced in professional contexts. I imagined a chorus of individuals and groups in cities or rural outposts, in theatres or at the kitchen table, in pubs and clubs, hospitals and community centres, schools and colleges, live or live-streamed, coming together across the world in a simultaneous celebration of diversity and what it is to be human. We already have our International Day of the Disabled Person on December 3rd... Perhaps now, with the publication of these texts, we are taking the first actions towards our own 'd' day...?

Kaite O'Reilly
Llanarth, Wales
1st August 2018

IN WATER I'M WEIGHTLESS
(2009 – 2012)

CONTEXT

In 2008 I was awarded a Creative Wales Award from Arts Council Wales to explore the form of the monologue. I had long held the ambition of creating a *body* of work specifically for atypical actors – the passed-over, neglected, often problematically represented. I decided to write monologues inspired by lived experience. Between 2009 and the present I have had over one hundred conversations and interviews with disabled and D/deaf people. In addition, I have received over fifty anonymous questionnaires exploring the respondents' dreams, hopes, imaginations, frustrations, identities and experiences – good, bad, and ugly. These confidences have inspired my fictional narratives, featuring alternative protagonists and alternative endings to the ones foregrounded in our public theatres and media.

The very first monologues were presented in 2009 script-in-hand at National Theatre Studio in London and The Unity Festival, Cardiff, performed by Sara Beer, Macsen McKay, Rosaleen Moriarty Simmonds and Maggie Hampton, directed by Phillip Zarrilli. An early version of *Walkie Talkies* was broadcast on BBC Radio 3 as part of the Freethinking Festival, performed by Mandy Colleran and directed by Justine Potter.

As the project developed, I received several Cultural Olympiad commissions and awards from Unlimited. *In Water I'm Weightless* became part of the official festival celebrating the 2012 London Olympics/Paralympics at Southbank Centre and Wales Millennium Centre, produced by National Theatre Wales (NTW).

When I presented the growing collection of *'d' Monologues* to John E McGrath, who directed the NTW premiere, he invited the cast – six of the UK's leading Deaf and disabled performers

– to select the texts to be performed. McGrath's radical process created an extraordinary dynamic and sense of ownership amongst the ensemble and our collaboration established the aesthetic of shared and collectively-told monologues I have been developing ever since. The playing order, dramaturgy, line assignment and edited texts from McGrath's production are published in *Atypical Plays for Atypical Actors* (Oberon, 2016). This serves as a useful template for the interested theatre maker, although I invite fresh re-makings and assemblages, where the order and dramaturgy of these texts find new montages, contexts, and imaginations.

What follows are the full, unabridged performance texts, plus previously unperformed monologues and excerpts from *I Fall To Pieces*, a solo performed as work-in-progress by Julie McNamara at DaDaFest in 2010, directed by Phillip Zarrilli.

An Unlimited commission for the Cultural Olympiad and London 2012 Festival, produced by National Theatre Wales at Wales Millennium Centre and Southbank Centre, *In Water I'm Weightless* premiered at WMC on 26th July 2012.

Director	John E McGrath
Producer	Lucy Davies
Designer	Paul Clay
Movement Director	Nigel Charnock
Associate Choreographer	Catherine Bennett
Emerging Director	Sara Beer
Cast	Mandy Colleran
	Mat Fraser
	Karina Jones
	Nick Phillips
	Sophie Stone
	David Toole
Sign language interpreters	Jo Ross
	Julie Hornsby
Visual language expert	Jean St Clair

*

Fragments on a Fragmentary Vision was my first piece of disability art, published in DAM – Disability Arts Magazine – in the early 1990s.

Reviews for the first production:

'…thrillingly vitriolic…' *The Guardian*

'…a powerful piece of theatre, shattering any stereotypes…a thought-provoking, beautiful piece of theatre which makes you realise that everyone is unique – and equal…' *The Western Mail*

'…What sets *In Water I'm Weightless* apart is that although disability is the topic of choice, the play transcends this… depict[ing] lives filled with emotion, circumstance and a vulnerability that everyman can identify with. This is a celebration of humanity, of the body, of character and resilience, in all forms…provocative and stimulating…' *The Public Reviews*

A SHORT HISTORY OF FEAR

I speak to you: the useless eaters, the mongs,
the spazzies, the shunned, the feared, those with
differently-abled limbs, minds, organs, senses,
those intellectually challenged by hate and
prejudice, not by brain circuitry. The schitzos,
the deafies, the crippled, the mad, bad, and
dangerous to know – I salute you – for by your
existence you threaten the narrow definition of
human variety, you broaden the scope of homo
sapien possibilities, you challenge normalcy, the
normative, Norm – and he hates you for it. You,
with the Stevie Wonder eyes, the Parkinson's
touch, the FDR shuffle and shake, your tush
proud and in that chair – let us carry you aloft
in your chariot, you marvel, you scientific
enigma, you medical conundrum, you gem of the
genome. O glorious freak of nature, let us cherish
you and lay tribute at your miraculous twisted
feet, you brittle beauty, boned like a Faberge egg,
precious one, unique.

You threatened, endangered species, let us save
you for future generations, you rare jewel of
genetic code, dodo diamond of DNA.

Do you know, even for one moment, how extraordinary you are? You are the wonders of the past, the Cyclops, the Minotaur – no wonder they feared you, with your capacity to be beyond what they could ever be, just by breathing.

You are the dragon of their folklore, the bogeyman of their chastising tales. No wonder they set out on crusades to destroy you – or, in later years, paid for the privilege to see you eat, walk, sleep, cry, turn your gorgon eye towards them, your own limbs already petrified, manacled to the walls in the dungeons of their asylums. No wonder they queued to watch you swallow down their disabling pills and pushed for front row seats at the performance of your lobotomy, you sedated but still awake, wide-eyed at the stab of the stiletto into your brain via an eye socket, this their brutal attempt to subdue your visions and appetites.

You, whose exquisite hands sculpt meaning into air, defying gravity and the root of all Indo-European languages: How they hate you for your visceral eloquence and synapse-firing brain so different from their own lit up language centres. No wonder they tried to destroy you and deny your existence, force your mouth to shape as

theirs, stamp on your culture and language as
they tied your tongue behind your back.

I speak to you, the rewired, reformed,
resuscitated, you six million dollared men and
women, they now have the technology to rebuild
you, but they will never surpass your audacious
evolution. You are both historic and forthcoming,
the monstered past and the cyborg future, O
Darth Vader of their nights and dreams, you
who breathe water and have oxygen piped to
your lungs, you molecular marvel who inhale
pharmaceuticals and cough out spume, you
amaze me. I am dazzled. I salute you all, you
definitive shock and awe, you mercurial mutants,
you species who both prove and disprove Darwin
– long may you continue, long may you thrive.

No wonder they feared you.

I'M SORRY

I'm sorry.

I'm so, so sorry. It will happen to you.

It will happen on a specific date at a fragmented hour and immediately everything you know will change.

It will happen slowly, so inconsequentially that you will not notice until a moment before it is upon you and there is nothing you will be able to do to avoid it.

It will happen in slow motion, in the second the metal of the car slams into the flesh of your body. The cells and the sinews and the crushed blood vessels and the synapses clicking and you going 'oh, oh,' knowing it has happened as you spiral and hit the tarmac, but still not really believing it – that horror, that churning horror as you realise it's not going to be a happy ending, after all.

There are no happy endings.

There are only endings.

But before the endings, sometimes a great length of time before the actual endings, there is the moment of change.

Sometimes it is swift and shrill and cunning – in on and away and nothing will be the same again.

Sometimes it is slow – so slow and slight the accumulation, you are not aware until it has passed the point of return – if ever there is a point from which return is possible. Once change happens, there's no going back, even if the previous state has seemingly returned. No. You have changed irrevocably by what your tissues have known, what the molecules have experienced. There is no return to innocence or inexperience.

I'm sorry, but it will happen to you in a moment's carelessness – the groping foot on the stair after one drink too many; the nudge from a passing stranger that knocks you off kilter and into the traffic, the thoughtless tuning of the radio which facilitates the impact at thirty miles an hour and them saying you came from nowhere and they didn't even see you.

It will happen by a dulling, slow and daily, over so many hours that perhaps friends and family will notice first, and you will deny it, seeing their creased foreheads and exchanged knowing eyes, angry with them and the ultimate betrayal – your own body turning against you.

It will happen suddenly one morning with the smell of burning rubber and the numbness of your feet on the cold bedroom floor, that worn, familiar patch now distanced, made new, unrecognisable.

It will happen in a heartbeat.

It will happen with the steady growth of moss on trees in a forest.

It will happen with the shrill immediacy of a siren starting up, landlocked in traffic.

It will happen.

I'm sorry. I don't know when it will happen, but it will happen to you.

It will.

I'm sorry.

It will happen.

WALKIE TALKIES

For Mandy Colleran and Nick Phillips

I'm a lucky kind of person. I'm blessed a lot.
I don't mean with the holy water at Lourdes (but
believe me, I've had a narrow escape from a few
of those outings…) I mean when people pass me
on the street. There's a little cluck of the tongue
and 'Bless, love her…' There I am, exalted again.
And people always seem to think I've no money.
'The poor thing…Bless…' Pitied and sanctified
in one sentence; amazing. These walkie talkies
must have very complicated emotional lives. But
they're very generous. I was having a drink and
a fag with some friends outside the pub the other
day – absconding from my 'Life Skills' class –
and someone put some coins in my tin of Special
Brew, and then got cross when I didn't have any
stickers. 'Well, give me something' they insisted,
and I said 'sorry, I don't believe in charity.
But thanks for the beer money. Next one's
on you. Cheers.'

I hope my luck's with me, today. I've got my
interview. They're all here: Mam and Dad, social
worker, occupational therapist, director of

the centre, the works. They think I'm daft, looking for the exit.

'Life's hard enough, why make it even more difficult?'

'Everything's laid on here, you're well looked after.'

'What are you going to do, stuck on your own in a flat all day?'

I don't know. But I'd like the opportunity to find out.

I think I'd run a long bath and float seductively in the bubbles, receiving visitors. We could sip lager, order pizza with extra garlic and the cheesy crust and eat dry roasted peanuts – they won't allow them in here, in case of an allergy. I'd buy a pair of crotchless knickers just because I could – and go to bed when I was tired, rather than when I was supposed to. I'd play music really loud – some awful death thrash metal, or Shostakovich – start looking for a job and ruminate on the nature of freedom. Some think it's a state of mind – like *Papillon*, that film about the wrongly imprisoned man who loved butterflies and tattooed one on his chest.

I'd like that. A tattoo. They, of course, wouldn't hear of it. 'Not appropriate,' they said. For what? For me to spend my Disability Living Allowance on? It's my money. Or not appropriate for me, full stop?

It's my body. Or so I like to think.

I fancy a great stonking Up Yours emblazoned
on my chest. Not literally. I mean symbolically.
Some beautiful, defiant symbol they'd look twice
at when stripping me for a bath. I hate that, their
jocular cheeriness. I know they're only trying
to help and avoid embarrassment, spare my
feelings, but I'm used to it and I like my privacy.

In water I'm weightless, like a mermaid – in my
own element, free to move. But they're scared
I'll drown – in two inches of water, which is all
they'll put in, despite my complaints.

But yes – something wonderful in hieroglyphics,
or Chinese script, embroidered on my skin;
something only I would know the meaning of:
I Am Me.
Or: 100% concentrate.
Good things come in little packages.
Or Poison. Yes, Poison. I like that.
Or maybe I'd just go for Liberty.

Of course I'd miss people from in here if I'm
successful with my plea, but they could always
visit.

There's Gerald, who communicates by blinking
and directing his eyes to an alphabet board. He's
saving up to have an electronic device, so he

can do Stephen Hawking impersonations when waxing lyrical about quantum physics, or string theory, or whatever else is going on in his head at any time. He's got an amazing brain. It's like all the energy that should have gone to the rest of his body got used up powering that astonishing mind of his, instead. He's an organic computer. Give him any equation and he whizzes away for a few seconds like a blender, then spends five minutes telling you what took him seconds to calculate. But it's always worth waiting for. That's what we do, work on a different time zone. Those walkie talkies are so impatient, always second-guessing what Gerald's saying, going at quark speed, then missing out on a nice little profit, like the dead cert for the 3.30 at Doncaster. We all made fifty quid – fifty quid towards Gerald's electronic voice box and fifty quid towards my running away fund. Maybe that should be my wheeling away and not bloody looking back once fund.

There – proof that patience is a virtue, just like the nuns told us, but also you can get your reward on earth, which is the opposite of what their holinesses said. We're doing our penance now, we were told, so it'd be straight through the pearly gates, no loitering in limbo like a load of chavs trying to get into a nightclub past the bouncers. I quite like that idea: impairment as an 'Access all Areas' pass – disability as a sort of celestial 'I'm with the band.'

I've made a good bit on the gee-gees thanks to Gerald, a little liferaft to help float me out of this place. He's a mathematical genius and knows the form, but most think that the lights aren't even on, never mind someone of brilliance being at home. It's weird how they think some are gifted – like John, who's visually impaired. He comes out with the biggest load of gobshite and there they all are, scooping up every syllable as they fall from his lips, lapping it up like he's said something meaningful. I think he's been labelled unfairly – I call him philosophically challenged. He's just asking if he needs a top-up in his tea when they come round with the urn, but they go all noddy-headed and attentive, their eyes on the distance, digesting. 'But is the cup empty or half full?' he yells in frustration and they sigh and pat his shoulder, thinking he's saying something profound about existence and perception.

They always think the blindies and viz imps have special powers – psychic, the mystical third eye opened – able to circumnavigate like bats by sonic hearing... No, they've just learnt the route across the dining room with such painstaking detail they can dash across for seconds and beat the rest of us. We wheelies sometimes put obstacles in their way to even the odds so we get there first. There's no open-mouthed wondering at special sonic awareness when there's bodies and spotted dick and custard on the floor, let me tell you.

But it's weird how they go – ignore geniuses like Gerald and tap into the more socially acceptable (to them) impairments – they always want us to say please and thank you and very little else. They love the tame ones – you know, who used to come out and dribble gratefully over Terry Wogan at Telethon, before our civil rights demonstrations put it off the air. Rights, not charity, too bloody right. That's going to be my argument for independent living – an expression of my civil liberties. But I have to be careful how I present it. They like the tame, pet crips. Me? I'm feral.

Nearly my time in, now. Got to get myself ready, psyche myself up: Ramp up the steps, rip away the doors, blow open narrow minds; give me my sovereignty, my self-determination, my autonomy.

And if they tell me I'll get into an awful mess without them to look after me, I'll just quote what Gandhi said when arguing for Indian independence: Yes, but at least it will be my mess. Because it's my life.

Isn't it?

BOY SOLDIER

For Macsen McKay, the original Boy Soldier.

Nelson lost one eye and a limb.
Napoleon had one arm and he was little and
probably epileptic.
Joan of Arc is said now to have had migraines or
petit mal. Some kind of seizures.
Almost all brilliant generals have been disabled.

An impairment gives you the edge, it means you
have to work harder, but you've less to lose.
Fear is smaller.
Pain can be a frequent companion, not something
to be warned with, or scared off from.
When you're in it and dealing with it, you
become invincible.

I go to a regular school.
Not like my parents who, back in the olden days
– when everything was in black and white – back
in the olden days my parents were considered
special.
But not in a good sense.
They went to a special school where they learnt
to play table football and say please and thank
you and became very good at macramé.

Or so dad says.

He pretends it's a joke, but I think he's bitter.

There's no need to be bitter when you can be strong.

Life isn't Disney Channel.

I hate those programmes where they use sick or disabled kids to pull at the heart strings.

There's always some boy with a shaved head

– Mummy's brave little soldier –

Let me tell you about soldiers.

Let me tell you what soldiers endure.

They take pain and splintered bone and risk and fear and they eat it for breakfast.

That brave little soldier doesn't need your sympathy.

He's twice the man you'll ever be.

I'm Welsh.

At the Eisteddfod the Druid asks, *'A oes heddwch?'*

'Is there peace?'

There is not peace.

Fe godwn ni eto.

The campaign continues.

I'm a soldier.

I'm a general.

I've an army

And we know where you live.

RANDOM GROWTH

When I was younger – teens, perhaps – people always asked me what I wanted to be when I grew up. 'Whole' I would say. 'A real, full girl/ boy' because being fragmented didn't feel *real* –or not real like the stories in soaps seemed real. 'Fragmented' as that's how I felt, even before I really knew the word or what it meant. I felt in fragments, missing something, lacking, without. I don't think I ever felt broken. *Broken* suggested you had all the pieces to begin with, and I came with parts missing, like flat pack furniture from Ikea. You know how it is when you cart it all home and spend forever putting it together with a variety of fiddly bolts in those splintery holes, tightened with strange, tiny spanners – and then it just slumps, or won't stand up properly on its own – has some kind of technical fault you need an expert to advise you on, or have to send it back, faulty, to the manufacturers. Well, I suppose it was like that when my exhausted and bewildered parents got me home in the Moses basket, still smelling of newness and hope and Mothercare. Only they couldn't return me to the faulty goods department. They had me. For good.

Disappointment is the word that springs to mind.
Not that my parents ever said such to me –
which, as a teenager, made me feel even more
fragile and apart. All my friends were having
great, operatic rows with their parents about how
disappointing they were as offspring, and they'd
never have gone to all that trouble and expense
of having them if they'd known for just one
second how they'd turn out.
Which was not a phrase my parents could ever
say to me, of course.
Even though I wished they would.
Even though they thought it –
I could tell.
You can smell disappointment.
It rises up like unwashed sheets in an unmade
bed.
So maybe that's what I was – unmade –
Or like my mother said when I was a child and
asked why I am as I am
'You just needed to stay a little longer in the oven,
sweetheart. You're not quite 'done' in the middle.'
I've often wondered what kind of food I might
have been:
A soufflé
Or baked Alaska.

Surely not a bun, or a loaf, that would be too clichéd – all kneady and blanched and soggy in the middle.

Maybe that's it.

Kneady. But without the 'k'.

SWITCH ON, SWITCH OFF

Spoken and visual language – VV or theatricalised British Sign language (BSL).

(spoken) It started with a desire to know what
the wind sounded like. When it rattles, or roars,
or whispers through the trees, like they say in
books. How can it do all those things? Whistle,
howl, screech, rustle… How can one wind do
so many things – or are there different winds? Is
this something you people know but mine don't?
Know the names and voices of different winds?
It *(signed) feels (spoken)* to me. It can be *(in BSL/
visual)* soft, silky, playful, chilly, rough, fresh.
(spoken) And what means *sound*, anyway?
I looked in a thesaurus: *(signed and spoken)* Noise.
Resonance. Hum. Echo. Thud. Reverberation.
Crash. Jingle. Swish. Clatter. Ring. Tinkle.
Jangle. Drone. Murmur. Buzz. Whizz. Whirr…
Those last words made me think of my washing
machine. I was exhausted.
(spoken) I questioned: Did I really want to join
this 'sound' world? How would you ever sleep?
Or work, read, concentrate, pass exams, have
a conversation with all that *(visual only)* bang
whoosh whirr thump bang knock *(spoken)* going
on? And did they really *sound* like that, or were

they just ways of animating the mouth for lip reading?

For the first few days, after, I did silly things – switch on and off the light – I never knew light had sound, before. It was short and quick and instant – maybe how it looked – dark and then light – dark and then light. Dark and then – I stood in the hallway, the tip of my finger bloodless as I… *(Demonstrates switching on and off a light switch: dark and then light, dark and then light; dark and then…)*

And my cat. That strange whatever you would call it. I don't know what to call it. You would know. It's frightening, like my cat swallowed a bee. And to speak like that is new: Before, I didn't know bees *noised. (Shows sign for 'bee' – then show the buzz: angry, dangerous – very different from lovely bee sign.)*

(spoken) I'm not sure I like this new world. It's violent, with sharp quick edges and I don't think it likes me very much, either.

RETREAT

For Phillip Zarrilli

Sometimes, sometimes I try to listen. I sink down
into my bones, my flesh, and imagine it like the
texture of a peach – sweet and ripe, firm, ready
for the picking. My inner organs, I mean. The
skin is an organ, the biggest in the body I'm told.
Laid flat, it would cover the size of a football field
– spread real thin, I guess.
But it's the inner organs. The spleen and the
liver and the bladder and the kidneys. The
oesophagus, the lungs. I all but forgot the heart.
The heart. And I try to listen and sometimes I
go even deeper and imagine I can feel a thought
forming – sense the electric impulse across the
chemical soup between the neurons – feel that
charge – the flicker of information (ticker-tape)
from one cell to the next. That's all it takes. One
cell. That's what begins it all.
And I wonder if that's how it began over three
billion years ago, the single celled algae, ancestor
of sponges and corals and trilobites. And the
mosses and dinosaurs and flowers and ape-men;
the dividing and sub-dividing, the multiplication
of it all, of life.

Only mine was in the negative.

A cell has no morality. It doesn't know if it is
good or bad. It is programmed solely to survive,
to increase, to grow, expand. It has brute
intelligence, like any expansionist force. It has
tactics, surprise ambushes, invasions in unlikely
places – a coup d'état that is secretive, silent,
lethal, effective.

It's strange when your very being is a warzone
carried out at molecular level. Visigoths and
Genghis Khan – the slaughter in the trenches –
massacre at Wounded Knee. I studied it all as a
boy – troop deployments, topography, artillery
locations, strategy; visited the battlefields of the
Civil War – Antietam, Chattanooga, Gettysburg,
site of Pickett's infamous 'charge' – saluted
the fabled dead: Lee, Sherman, Jackson – yet
believed I was immortal.

Like everyone, I guess.

For this is what it is to be human, to be animal:
to weaken, get sick; the slackening, the ebbing of
strength, the indignity, the stripping of disease.

And I thought why me?

And I thought why not?

Why not me alongside the scarf wearing women,
defiant slash of war paint like blood across their
mouths; the men camouflaging their catheters

with shy smiles and draped dressing-gowns, the
spectre-thin children, already haunting their
parents' eyes. Why not me as I sit with the others,
a cup of tea in our laps and bag of poison in
our veins, wondering how it can tell the white
hats from the black, wondering of the innocent
casualties through friendly fire, sensing the singe
of devastation, the Blitzkrieg shock and awe, that
fleshy Dresden, wondering whose side is it on?
And for me the battle died down – just a trace
of smoke in my nostrils, a buzzing in my blood,
the taste of metal in my mouth and the guilt
of surviving.
Then nothing.
No D Day. No surrender. No peace treaty. Just a
retreat. Final or temporary? No one knows.
So sometimes I find myself listening – sinking
down into the old territory, listening for sniper
fire, distant drums, for a sign just one sign, a sign
from one cell

        that it will soon be all over.

FRAGMENTS ON A FRAGMENTARY VISION

Columbus got it wrong. The world is flat. Without dimension, but such colour, shapes.

How do we describe seeing?

Definition: See. Verb. Have or use power of perceiving with eye; descry; observe; look at; discern mentally; be passive spectator of.

My sight is not passive. It is maverick, flattening the world with a stroke of the retina. Buildings fall into straight lines at my glance; at my mercurial eye the earth trembles. Like Lear, I strike flat the thick rotundity of the world.

I walk down the road, not knowing if the car before me is moving or stationary.
I walk down the road with my bird-like cranings
– the tilt of the jerking head, the eye monitoring, deceiving, explaining, deciphering.
Was that a black cat or just a blind spot crossing my path? Forever optimistic. A cat, it was. I will be in luck today.
No, it was a manhole, uncovered. I fall down.
I will still be in luck today.

How do we describe seeing?

A rock lying on the beach. I touch its surface,
marvelling as my fingertips discover contour,
structure, space. The shadows of it I colour with
my roughened hands. I see feelingly.

Definition: Fragmentary. Broken (Latin fragmantum;
French, frangere, to break)

My sight is not broken. It is clear. Pure. Shards of
vision, of light, converged in my mind's eye.

My sight is not broken. Rather, it breaks the
world.

My love is tenderloined and all-sighted. He flicks
through the world, jack-knifing corners, skinny-
hipping crowds. He crows through the balls of his
feet, suspended in perpetual motion.
I carve him, carve him with my fingers, sculpt
him from the hard, flat stone. Bones hide below
the surface, becoming alive, rushing upwards to
meet my hands.

See how your features bloom beneath my hands!
Your bones take shape, rising to greet me,
becoming animated, breathed of life, you come
from the flat screen into dimension with my
fingers.

*Definition: Flat: horizontal, level, not curved or
rounded or sharp; unqualified, dull, dejected, without
effervescence, insipid, stale.*

I redefine my flatness.
My sight redefines the wor(l)d.

JAW JAW JAW JAW JAW JAW

In visual language – no voice.

All around me people are chewing air.
Jaw jaw jaw jaw jaw jaw jaw
After a while, it hurts the eyes.
They do it in pairs, and in groups, but most
alone, hand to ear[1], on the bus, in the street, on
the train, in shops.
What can be so important?
What is happening that demands this constant
Jaw jaw jaw jaw jaw jaw?
Is it something I don't know?
Is the world ending?
Have they just discovered the meaning of life and
have to share it with everyone they know before
they forget?
Jaw jaw jaw jaw jaw jaw
They are eating the planet.
Gobbling it up.
There will be nothing left
but a huge mouth, grotesque,
MASTICATING
Jaw jaw jaw jaw jaw jaw.

Mouths are for kissing.

---

1   Mobile phone

BEG

We're supposed to crave contact.
I don't.
I like distance, space,
room around me to breathe.
I've been undressed too many times
 – roughly –
not out of urgency, or eagerness
– desire –
just rush.
Clothes yanked over my head. Buttons and flies
undone
and I'm not even there.
They might as well be undressing a corpse
– solid air –
they don't see me.
They might even be chatting to someone in
another room and I'm just
a chore,
an entity to be stripped, examined, washed,
dressed, or put to bed.
That's why you're not allowed to touch me.
You may crave it.
You might even beg.
So go on then: beg.
Beg. Beg for me.

Beg.

You know you'd never experience anything else quite like it.

No one else quite like me.

So go on.

I know you want to.

I can see your eyes.

Go on:

Beg.

LUVVIES –

I'm always playing zombies. The sick and twisted
psycho. I suppose it's better than being one
of the Magnificent 7 – and I'm talking Snow
White here, not Yul Brynner. What I'd give
to be 'Wo/man 1'. That's it, just 'Wo/man 1'.
Or 'Neighbour 3'… 'Fish and chip customer'
on *EastEnders*… Even 'waiting patient' in some
hospital drama – you know, some poor love with
a makeshift bandage over their eye… But – no…
No… No bit part for me. I always have to be the
star attraction: The ghoulish complication that
has the doctors scratching their heads or each
other's eyes out. Whether it's a horror flick or
not, I'm always the monster. The experiment
gone horribly wrong. The accident people flinch
at when first meeting. The misunderstood evil
genius, just wanting a bit of love – or my personal
favourite: the plot device.
I did a crip' cameo on a cop show the other
week, leading a demonstration about the pig
pen not being fully accessible. It was storylined
by a wheelchair-using writer on an equal opps,
inclusive, cultural diversity attachment.
My character was protesting it was every disabled
person's right to be treated like a criminal.

Fantastic. I smashed a few windows, broke the peace, was arrested for assaulting a WPC and then proved my point, as they couldn't take me down into the cells because of the stairs.

It was nice, playing a human. I hadn't done that since a mini-series for the Beeb to commemorate yet another anniversary of the First World War.

I was playing an ambulance driver on the Front who went over a landmine…

You get the picture.

Typecast again.

THINGS I HAVE LIP READ

Visual and spoken/projected language

What a pity, their mouths say, she's deaf and dumb.
And so pretty, too.
But at least that's something; she has her looks.
And she can be deep and mysterious, or look pretty
on an arm, or a bar stool, or helping in the kitchen.
Some men like quiet.
Some men prefer women who are like Victorian
children:
Seen, but not heard.
At least she won't nag.
At least she won't drive you spare with her chatter
the moment you come in through the door from
work.
At least she won't ask you what you're thinking
when your mind's blank and you're vegetating, just
watching the TV.
And the phone bill will be small.
And she won't be asking you if you love her just
after the main event.
And if she cries, it won't wake you up.
And she won't always have the last word in an
argument.
There'll be no shouting matches, no recriminations.
She'll keep herself to herself and be grateful.

And express herself by what she does.

After all, actions speak louder than words.

Put like that, it's a pity more women aren't like her.

YOUR TONGUE, MY LIPS

–   Shiny buckles polished to a glint.
    Leather. Stiff. Pliant, like skin.

–   He called me doll face.

–   The snap of strict leather, biting, the yawn of
    the corset's pink tongue across my midriff, my
    nether, my body, my waist, tongue, my midriff,
    my nether, my body, my waist... *(Loop.)*

–   Lower. Yes, there.
    Ozone. Fingers trailing. Breath. Breath. Breathe.
    Breath. Pungent. The ache. The yearning. The
    salve. Sliding through the water, ocean's depth.
    The nibble of mouths. Ozone breath   when
    your fingers are on   in   the yearning the heat
    the soldering touch   the melt and ache
    the yawn   the mouth blood-warm blood-rich
    the yielding   the meeting   the melting
    the melding   the joining   the

–   Come lie with me.
    I'm all metal and pins.

–   He called me doll face.
    I hated dolls.
    They took me to a child's psychologist for
    mutilating my toys, butchering my dolls,

shortening their arms, their legs. I just wanted
something that reflected me. In a world of bodies
unlike my own, I wanted, as a child, something
that looked like me.

–   Waist-high in the world.
    Eye level, the crotch.
    Well, that's handy, s/he said.
    Can you do it? S/he asked.
    I mean, have you the wherewithal?
    The you know. Equipment.

–   The nibble of mouths. The slide   the slip
    the ozone breath   when your fingers are on   in

–   Is it all in working order? Shipshape?
    Water tight? Ready for servicing?

–   Everywhere there's men.

–   Is it all in top notch working condition, or can't
    you?
    What I mean is, can you do it?
    You do have one, don't you?
    Is it active?
    Does it respond?
    Does it work?

–   It

–   Your todger. Dongle. Meat and two veg.

The family jewels. Your sausage. Love hammer.
Sex chisel. Moan machine.

- I'm sorry

- Love truncheon, trouser snake, light sabre, sword
  of Damacles, wanger, schlong, magic wand, cock-
  a-doodle-doo!

- When I was a child I was told my front bottom
  was evil. It was a sinister place to be respected
  and feared and no one or nothing – least of all
  my fingers – should ever go there, or they'd be
  bitten off by the huge sharp teeth.

- I'm sorry

- Your wotsit your thingy your

- Everywhere there's men.
  On the bus, in the street, in cafes, on the tube,
  Cycling by in lycra, plums in a taut bag – fruit to
  be picked, squeezed, pressed against the mouth –
  I'm dirty.
  I'm very, very dirty – you need to take a shower
  after just thinking of me.

- Sorry

- I like it best when it hurts.

And with my body, made of pain
it hurts all the time.

So who's a lucky girl, then?

ACT AS IF

Act as if nothing is wrong and you're fine.
Act as if they know something and might actually
help you.
You think of the waste – all the taxpayer's money
going for you to sit around in someone else's
clothes, having a terrible time, not getting
any better.
You should try harder.
You can't bear to think of all that money going
to waste.
You've come here, you're taking up their valuable
time, so you should tell them, tell them what the
matter is.
You open your mouth and it comes out – is this
what they want? Is the voice telling the right
stories?
Is this what they need to fix what's wrong and
make you better? Have you performed right?
Given him all the right cues?
And then you realise it's just an ageing man with
a cup of coffee gone cold beside him, who knows
nothing. Like you, he's keeping up the pretence.
Act as if. Once you both stop believing in his
magic, his knowledge, it's just a man and a wo/
man sitting in the interior of a room – unlived

in, but pretending, like a film set – and it's never
going to get better otherwise, so you try and
make yourself believe.

Yes, doctor. Whatever you think is best, doctor.
And you're out in the corridor with a diagnosis
and prescription for three types of sedatives in
your hands.

But you know all this. You know the story. You've
seen it in enough documentaries and mini-dramas
on TV.

But what's different is the ease with which it can
happen.

And to you.

THIS IS HOW MADNESS BEGINS

This is how madness begins:
Beautifully, but with euphoric pain.

This is how madness begins:
With the smell of roses and Technicolor
brightness and the surge of blood inside the veins.

This is how madness begins:
With a couple of late nighters which extend into
a week with no sleep, no change of clothing, no
food, plenty of alcohol.

This is how madness begins:
With a chemical imbalance formed in the womb.

This is how madness begins:
With the death of a lover, the birth of a child, the
last illness of a parent.

This is how madness begins:
With the knowledge everything dies and
therefore everything is utterly futile.

This is how madness begins:
With clarity and understanding of
the hidden truth in all things.

This is how madness begins.

CHORUS

Thank you so so much for patronising me and denying me my human rights. You're absolutely right, why would I need civil liberties? I don't need to work, to contribute, to be independent, part of society, social life. Yes, we are fire hazards, and such an expensive drain with our demands for ramps, and equality, and access to work and public buildings like schools and nightclubs, supermarkets and cinemas. The politicians are right; we shouldn't be left to fester. Make those cuts and save the taxpayers money. Put us back behind the walls, into the homes, the families, the institutions. Make us invisible again and we'll just be grateful.

DELILAH

So here I am in Morrisons, strapped to a customised shopping trolley with rocket launchers and a mouth-operated SA80 machine gun mounted on the kiddy seat. I'm 'Delilah The Flesh Eating Lesbian Bandit Queen'…or at least that's what they told my agent.

It's not clear what my character's sexual orientation has to do with the dramatic action, so I asked the floor manager: 'Greg, if you're on cans, can you speak to the director and clarify something for me? It says 'lesbian' in the script, but as there's no actual Sapphic activities scripted, should I try and suggest my 'bohemian lasciviousness' by how I lick Woman Shopper 3's face before tearing her cheek away? Or are we going for suggestion here? Is 'lesbian' literal, subtext, or just part of my backstory?'
So we're waiting to find out.

I saw them – the other actors – roll their eyes when I asked the question, but it's important. I like to know what the director's after and I do have a reputation for being professional. I am the consummate professional, all the way down to my thirteen toes…

That always gets the attention. They presume I've
been playing in Make-up with the nose putty and
I've lost count of the times some runner has tried
to pull off my feet, or body-searched me, to find
where I've hidden my arms…

So it's: Me: 'Surprise!' and them: 'You're real!'

Over the years I've notched up more than
the occasional faint, which is probably why
I'm so in demand. I'm the Real Deal, what's
problematically known as 'authentic'.

But only 'problematic' from an academic point
of view… I learnt that when playing a scientist
whose time travel experiment had gone terribly
wrong, transporting my limbs into the distant
future whilst my torso remained in 1939. In
Vienna. Just in time for Josef Mengele to goose-
step in with all those nasty experiments…

Which reminds me, did you know Thalidomide
may have been created by the Nazis as an
antidote to nerve gas? It may not have been
discovered via an antihistamine gone wrong in
1954 after all, but potentially the last war crime
of the Third Reich… So let's put that in our
collective compensation pipe and smoke it.

But I digress. I'm here: strapped to a shopping trolley in Carmarthen…

These horror flicks are alright, but it's all spectacle and early starts with hours and hours in Make-up. What I'd give for the ease of a walk-on part… Not literally. I'm not prepared to use prosthetics again. They hurt. Well, you try putting your body weight down on what feels like broken glass. Repeatedly. Whilst trying to act 'normal' – whatever that is… And frankly, in my experience, they just get in the way. I've lost count of the times we've stopped traffic when Des – that's my partner – has pulled off my legs and slung them over his shoulder before flinging me into the back of an inaccessible taxi after a night on the lash.

So no, no bit part for me. I always have to be the focus of attention, the swell in dramatic music, the fearful thing behind a closed door… And then there's always the Polish cleaner who comes through the gaping curtains with her antiseptic wet-wipe – in she enters, all Polish or East European-y, with a sad and slightly sordid illegal immigrant subtext going on… and then she'll see me, genuflect and bless herself, saying something incomprehensible in her peasant language, which will remind all the viewers at home of the crowds storming the castle of Dr Frankenstein in gloomy Transylvania, or some such… And then out comes the burning torches, or the meat cleavers, AK-47s, or whatever contraption the writers have decided to torture me to death with this time, and I die screaming in a pool of ketchup and raspberry jelly, then go home, hoping it goes straight to DVD.

There are, of course, those who disagree with what I do for a living. Some things, I'm told, should be kept in the dark. *Thing* – they don't even merit me as human. Which is why, I suppose, I'm so successful in the supernatural genre. I must be the work of Satan, the devil himself, for God makes us in his likeness – or so these letters I get tell me – and have I looked at myself in a mirror recently? And one thing they know for certain, the lord Jesus certainly had four limbs, otherwise how else could they have hammered him onto that wooden cross?

I don't know about the son of god, but I feel crucified myself sometimes. I'm a martyr to extremists. Maybe that should be 'target'. And I don't just mean the letters, but I'm not allowed to talk about that. Sorry. What I *can* say without potentially prejudicing the jury is disability hate crime is definitely on the rise. So it's good to keep busy. It does no one any favours to barricade yourself in at home, afraid to go out because of what the trolls and all are threatening to do to you. And it's just as well I'm a firm believer in negatives being made into positives. Like my old acting coach used to say: 'You have to work with what you've got, darling, mine your personal experience for Acting Gold.'

So I do. Even here, strapped to a supermarket trolley in West Wales.

AFTER THE OPERATION

Performed in spoken and visual language.

(spoken and signed) 'You're jumpy', my girlfriend
said and we both jumped, me at the sudden
noise, and her at the shock of being heard. 'I keep
forgetting you can hear me', she said, her voice
still a surprise and *(signed) still a disappointment.*
(spoken) It's *(signed) thin and weak and flat (spoken)*
and I expected *(signed) full and rich and musical
and beautiful.*
(spoken) 'I never had you down as the neurotic
type.'
She'd never used that tone of face with me,
before.
'You used to be better than diazepam:
(signed and spoken) a happy pill on legs. It was
your U.S.P. *(spoken)* and what attracted me to you
in the first place.'
*(signed) She'd never used that tone of face with me,
before.*
(spoken) I haven't been able to sleep well since
the operation. I lie awake in bed. Before, I would
dream – slide into sleep like *(signed and spoken)*
getting into a bath of warm water all *(signed)*
dreaming, smiling, relaxed…

(signed and spoken) In water I'm weightless,
(signed) like a mermaid – in my own element, free
to move. (spoken) Now *(signed) I lie awake, wide-eyed*
in terror (spoken) hearing *(signed) robbers…ghosts…*
wild animals with big teeth (signed and spoken)
waiting to be slaughtered in my bed.
I wish the doctor had warned me.
Sound ambushes.
(signed) It creeps up and taps my shoulder like the
children's game Grandmother's Footsteps. It pounces,
close to the ear; it bounces screaming out of the doorbell,
or the phone, or a once gently vibrating alarm clock.
It tweets like a chatty budgie when the batteries on the
fire alarm are low, comes yelling round corners, jetting
across the sky, roaring down the road
(signed and spoken) and I'm cautious and nervous,
waiting for the next attack.
(spoken) I liked it better when my house didn't
groan. I liked my home when it was silent bricks
and mortar, before it started to complain.
And then just as I'm *(signed) dropping off to sleep*
– I'm woken by my blood itself, pulsing (spoken)
my blood pulsing through my ear as I rest my
head on the pillow *(signed) ticking – (spoken)* it
sounds like my body's *ticking* – the winding down
mechanism of life itself.
Sound makes you aware of your mortality.

(signed and spoken) You can hear that doomsday
clock in your blood. 'You're getting morbid,' my
girlfriend said.
I've decided hearing is
(signed then spoken) existential.

1 I have a tea ceremony.
   I rinse the cups and pot with boiling water, then
   add the leaves – teabags are so plebeian – and
   cover the pot with a cosy, leaving the tea to
   draw… What? I've always wondered. What
   picture would the tea draw? An Indian landscape
   filled with terraces and tea bushes and smiling
   women in jewel-coloured saris joyfully picking
   the tips, bangles jangling on their arms? Or is that
   just the advertisement?
   By the time I've thought this the tea has brewed
   and I pour some into the warmed cups – having
   rinsed them again, for luck, in the boiled water
   from the kettle – it's fragrant and amber coloured
   against the white china of my cups – always use
   cups, not mugs, they're so clumsy and common
   – then I add a dash of milk or sometimes lemon,
   depending on my mood. Biscuits arranged in an
   overlapping pattern like fish scales on the plate
   and then I go to the door, kneel, put the tray
   down, slide open the door, step through with
   the tray, kneel, put the tray down, pull the door
   closed, shuffle forward on my knees, placing the
   tray at precise right angles to her feet, exactly as
   I've learned from watching the Japanese foreign

language films. I try to smile like a geisha – eyes demure and lowered, teeth bright, face white and leadened. Then we begin our little ritual.

And how are you today?

Fine.

Do you have anything to tell me?

No.

The cup and saucer passed over so confidently – look, no spilling, no shaking, the tremor has all but gone.

Any dizziness?

No.

Really? I just wondered…the way you came in through the door…?

Oh, that was deliberate, I say. *Planned. It shows respect and decorum.*

And she gives me that kind of look.

I've seen it on television, I say, *and you said last time I should get a hobby, or interest outside myself, to broaden my horizons, so…?*

We smile and we sit – or, rather, she sits, her thighs loose and fallen apart in the low armchair, me kneeling, buttocks pertly placed on heels before her, head lowered, slightly angled, smile fastened, showing compliance and deference to her.

So. How's it been?

Fine, I say.

Any incidents?

Her hand stretches out for a biscuit, hovering over the pile, deciding where to break the shape and make a chink in the armour, hobnobs overlapping like chainmail. She takes one from the rim, sliding it out from under the others, leaving the pattern almost intact, almost undisturbed. I smile, appreciating her gesture. She knows things like that are important to me.

So. Any incidents, or 'episodes'?

She says the word meaningfully, except she's trying to undermine the significance of the term by dunking the hobnob into the tea. Filthy habit. And I'm saying

I'm sorry, you'll have to speak up, as I can't hear you. Speak louder. I can't hear you. I can't hear you for the shrieking inside my own head. What? I can't hear. Why do you always go on about it? I don't want to talk about it. Why do you always want to talk about it?

And that's it. That's the moment I know.

I try to regain my composure – I make a little laugh like it was a joke, like the Japanese lady, so controlled on television. I wait with my demure smile for the rejoining polite smile but it doesn't come. The fragile white china cup is banged down – it jangles – tea slopped into the pristine

saucer and she's writing something, her biro –
why can't she use a fountain pen? – her cheap
biro scrawling across the sheet, the noise rasping,
her pressure marking the words through not just
one sheet, but all the other papers like a scar, a
Braille through the entire file, indelible, marked
down for ever and that's the moment I know
– despite all my efforts, the practice, the dress-
wearing, the lipstick application, the mascara
brush licking cautiously at my lashes – I know
that I've failed; I'm not the woman they want –
the fragrant softly-spoken lady who can make
tea and have light bantering conversation over
hobnobs, her hair set, her best face on, and it's
not me, it's never been me, it will never be me,
despite all my efforts, the rehearsals, all my line
learning, the costume-wearing – the geisha mask
has slipped and there's

Me. Me. Me.

2   The Chinese believe that before you conquer a
beast, you first must make it beautiful.

Welcome to the beauty parlour.

The dayroom of one of the women's wards –
some standing dead still, others laughing inanely,
or screaming, or braiding their hair, or staring
with eyes which could suddenly go dead. The

agitated pacing, the Parkinson tremor, side effect
from medication, the pills that make you talk too
much, too loud, too loosely, or not at all. You'll
see someone moon-walking up the corridor, their
limbs alien, as though belonging to someone
else. A trail of tea stains across another's lap –
the distance from cup to lip unreachable without
first spilling half the contents, the machinegun
rat-a-tat-tat which, drug-induced, seizes the
elbow. Someone there half naked, paused in
the act of dressing – this suspension mid breath
– too stoned not to smile – the dropsy hands,
the drooping eyelids, the mumbling mouth, the
numbing. No dreams in this dreaming place.
The medication is effective.
Who wants to spend their life sedated?

3   At nights you hear them crying at lights out –
or banging their fists, if they weren't strapped
down, on the iron doors.
Iron doors. I could never understand why they
went for that. I'd never seen them, before, in any
other part of a hospital... I suppose it's fireproof –
an iron door – and better than wood for endlessly
throwing yourself against until a skull is cracked
or unconsciousness comes.
Did you believe that? Did you think that story
was true?

Did you think it was my story?

Did it give you a flush of titillation, or a little shiver through you with a whispered 'thank god they're locked up and away from me'?

Did you think of them like body snatchers, walking around like the rest of you – unrecognisable. They could be sitting beside you – or three rows back, two seats to the left – and you'd only ever know when they began frothing or screaming...

Is that what you think?

Or was it more Gothic – the madwoman locked away in the attic, humming to her own deranged tune, only getting her comeuppance burning to death when the house goes up over a careless candle and everyone's forgotten her until they're safe outside, bundled in blankets, breath cloudy in the midnight frost and there! There – her bare, bloodied arms reaching through the jagged glass between the bars on the windows...

Are those your associations?

I'm sorry, am I making you uncomfortable?

You shouldn't be.

It's all our fears, isn't it? To come away at the seams, to fall apart, to come unstuck – such physical, active descriptions – to crack up, to break down, to collapse, to go to pieces. To go

round the bend, up the wall, off your rocker,
away with the men in white coats.

It's a journey – you're moving away from the
known and familiar to an unspecified destination.
But it's precarious – you've lost control, lost your
head, lost all sense, lost your marbles along with
the will to live. You have a screw loose, have
become unhinged.

They're interesting, metaphors.
Ways to explain and describe something.
And there's always more than one, because
nothing is completely definable, knowable.
Beautiful words describing different things.
To be interpreted as the case demands.
And this is my case.
But you mustn't believe me, as all I say is true.

(Sings.) Crazy…I'm crazy for being so lonely
Crazy…Crazy for feeling so blue……
…I'm crazy for trying and I'm crazy for crying
And I'm crazy for

My condition is congenital.
I'm a congenital liar. I was born a storyteller,
a fabulist, a fabricator of tales. It's all invented,
anyway, reality.
It's made-up, interpreted in our brains.
It's all fiction.

Even this.

Someone else other than me wrote these words
I'm saying now.

Yes.

Even this.

Right now.

Really.

Maybe my doctor wrote it as a prescription.

Maybe I wrote it for my doctor.

Maybe she wrote it for me as my doctor.

Diagnosis is all narrative. A conclusion drawn
from analysis of other comments or words written
by people other than myself in a file labelled 'me'.
We're all hot-wired for stories. The myths of
creation, medical narratives, morality tales with a
warning – they're all the same – fiction, informed
by good intentions and a kind of 'truth' – to
make sense of the confusing, often random and
unconnected facets that make a universe, that
make a diagnosis, that make a life.

And it's all based on elusive, slippery, intangible,
non-empirical words.

Telling tales. Fabrication.

Well-meaning lying.

Can you explain to me the difference?

richard iii redux
(2018)

Historically few disabled performers have had the opportunity to play any part on the stage, however stereotypical, whilst leading disabled character roles have largely been the preserve of celebrity actors. It seems that physical or neuro-diverse transformation is still perceived as the pinnacle of actorly challenge and skill, an opinion reflected in the industry, which is why playing a crip' as a non-disabled thesp' is invariably an award-winning role.

The non-disabled actor's Everest is surely Shakespeare's *Richard III*, a part to relish deforming and making as individually monstrous as possible. And in *richard iii redux* we have deconstructed them all, from Olivier's nasal psychopath to Spacey's leg-braced Gaddifi, McKellen's black shirted fascist to Sher's double-crutched 'bottled spider,' Cumberbatch's life-like prosthetic to Eidinger's cushion-hump and clown shoe in Ostermeier's post-dramatic production…

We're not saying *Richard III* should never be performed by someone who isn't disabled, nor are we censoring or bowdlerising the Bard. Phillip Zarrilli and I both have great fondness for old 'crook-back'. What we seek to do with *richard iii redux* is to provide an alternative disability perspective in response to Shakespeare's construction of evil on the disabled body. And having a bit of fun as we do it.

I have known performer/collaborator Sara Beer since the 1980s when we were both involved in the Disabled People's Movement and the emerging disability arts and culture scene. Sara was the obvious choice for this project when I first conceived the idea of a one woman show about *Richard III* from a disability perspective, performed by someone with the same physicality as the historical Richard. It wouldn't be the first time a disabled actor has played the part. Mat Fraser played the title role in Northern Broadside's 2017 production, but given how monstrous Shakespeare's Richard is, and how far he deviates from historical accounts, I started questioning whether having a disabled actor play a distorted disabled part would be 'enough'? Would it create diversity and balance, or simply reinforce notions of 'normalcy' and negative representations of difference? Out of these questionings with co-creator and director/producer Phillip Zarrilli, the project emerged. This would not be a production of Shakespeare – rather, a response to Richard's portrayal both in Shakespeare's text and through the actors who have embodied him, viewed through a lens which is female, disabled, and predominantly Welsh.

Phillip Zarrilli is a renowned scholar, director, and actor-trainer, and so has brought a wealth of knowledge about acting to the production. We've been joyously irreverent, deconstructing the process of acting itself, as well as the process of creating a character. This expertise has enabled Sara Beer to play various fictional personas in a variety of accents, taking the audience on three simultaneous journeys in response to Shakespeare's *Richard III*:

– a child's self-awakening as she unexpectedly finds 'herself' IN Shakespeare,

– a professional performer's journey toward playing Richard, and

– a personal journey through Wales in search of the historical 'Richard' on the route to Bosworth Battlefield.

It was only after Phillip shared his historical research on the 'real' Richard III that I realised just how revised Shakespeare's hatchet job is. Just as black figures have been white-washed or erased from history, disabled figures have been either normalised or transformed into the hideous, fearful Other – and in Richard, we have character-assassination of the highest order.

It's a double-whammy. Not only did Shakespeare exaggerate Richard's atypical embodiment and contort it to represent evil, he also re-wrote history, transmuting a reforming, popular King who led thousands into battle despite his scoliosis, into an evil, murdering coward, ready to give up his kingdom for a horse (contemporary sources state he was offered a horse to flee the battlefield, but he responded his fate would be decided there – either to die at Bosworth, or live as King). It comes perhaps as no surprise that many consider *Richard III* as a piece of Tudor propaganda, written to please powerful patrons and reiterate their (tenuous) claim to the throne – the descendants of whom still live in the big palaces now.

The full title of our work is *richard iii redux OR Sara Beer [is/ not] richard iii*, but our subtitle doesn't need to remain attached in any future productions with other atypical actors. I propose putting the name of the actor into a new surtitle.

Playwrights have little power, but one we do have is deciding who can perform our words. As a counter to the tradition of 'cripping up' in Shakespeare's *Richard III*, we offer the rights to this text solely to the atypical performer: those who identify as disabled.

Produced by The Llanarth Group, supported by Arts Council Wales, *richard iii redux OR Sara Beer [is/not] richard iii* by Kaite O'Reilly and Phillip Zarrilli, premiered at Chapter Arts Centre, Cardiff, on International Women's Day, March 8th 2018.

Cast	Sara Beer
	Phillip Zarrilli (as PRESENTER)
Director/Producer	Phillip Zarrilli
Videographer	Paul Whittaker
Set/Costume Design	Deryn Tudor
Lighting Design	Joe Fletcher
Sound Design	Sam Jones
Stage Manager	Jacqui George
Translator	Carri Munn

*

The main performer plays various personas:

SERIOUS ACTOR

NATIONAL TREASURE

FICTIONALISED 'SELF' IN FAKE AUTOBIOGRAPHY

The PRESENTER is on video.

*

Each scene begins with a title projected onto a screen built into the set. The text is captioned throughout.

Reviews for the first production:

'It's really funny. I mean, very, very funny… *richard iii redux* is an insightful piece of disability art, mixing demonstrably excellent work by disabled people with biting social comment. More than this, it lets us into a new Richard, one free of disabling barriers.'
Disability Arts Online

'…excellent…captivating…confirmed by the loud, loving, standing ovation.' *Theatre-wales.co.uk*

'…unpredictable…evokes laughter and reflection in equal measure…intimate…witty…ingenious…commanding and nuanced…thought-provoking…uncompromisingly funny…has great power and impact…' *Arts Scene in Wales*

'…a bold, informative, occasionally traumatic, and irreverently amusing seventy minutes of theatre.' *British Theatre Guide*

(1) WHAT SEE YOU HERE, NOW?

SERIOUS ACTOR:

What see you here, now, before you?

Am I a dissembler? An ac-tor…

Or am I the 'thing itself'?

The one and self-same Richard, Duke of

Gloucester?

I stand here before you…duplicitous,

doubly duplicitous

both seeming to be what I am not,

and being what I am.

I am blasphemous…

subverting the proper 'order' of 'proper'

playing…

But I will not play proper with you and before

you.

Rather I shall 'play' you…dis-order you…un-pick

you…

I…one of those from the margins, the shadows,

come here now to stand before you

and re-claim what is mine-own,

this crooked shape,

this self-same body

that has been taken from me and mine.

Formed, twisted, rudely stamp'd by He-himself

as one 'not shaped for sportive tricks,

Nor made to court an amorous looking-glass…'
One 'curtail'd of…fair proportion,
Cheated of feature by dissembling nature'
and so deprived of 'love's majesty.'
He marks me a 'bottled spider…
A poisonous bunch-back'ed toad.'
'Deform'd, unfinish'd, sent before my time
Into this breathing world, scarce half made up,
And that so lamely and unfashionable
That dogs bark at me as I halt by them…'
Woof woof.
He marks me 'subtle, false, and treacherous'…
a murderer of heirs,
demands I 'prove a villain'.
Shall *I* a villain be?

'To be…or not to be,' Richard…' *that* is *my*
question'.

(2) STORIES AT NAN'S: 'ACTING'

FICTIONALISED AUTOBIOGRAPHY:

I always wanted to be an actor when I was little. That, or to join the Bay City Rollers on tour, dressed in mid-calf flared trousers with the little tartan turn-ups and yellow and black piping down the side… Mid 70's Rollermania… I so wanted to be part of the tartan army, sewing strips of *carmine, red oxide* and *white smoke plaid* to my clothes – even the names of the colours were romantic – a tartan skinny scarf around my raised wrist, shang-a-lang-ing along with Les McKeown…

But the nearest I got was waving my feet in time to the music as we lay on our tummies in the children's ward, watching *Top of the Pops* through the mirrors they gave us to see the telly. When you're in an abdominal plaster cast there's not a lot you can do except lie there on your front and wave your legs in the air. You can't go to school, so the teacher comes to you, and lessons – along with meals – are taken in the same position – flat on your tummy, legs in the air… no wonder we all got chronic indigestion. And we did crafts – lots and lots of crafts – with felt and glue and in my case yards of tartan ribbon, bought by the half mile from Woolworths – and when anyone went to cry, or was homesick for their mother, I told them of my secret life, of the adventures I had when they were all asleep and I was smuggled out of the ward and onto the tartan tour bus, serenaded by Les who knew our love was impossible and just couldn't be, and so every time he sang *(sings)* 'Bye bye baby, baby good bye…' – it was to me.

I think that was when the desire to act was seeded in me – from the power of stories to make people feel better – or perhaps it was just to make people *feel*. There was so much avoidance of emotion in our house: *'less said soonest mended,'* my Nan said, sitting at the head of the kitchen table overseeing the ritual of the pouring of the tea like an Egyptian deity, all hollowed cheekbones and bulging headdresses from the scarves she tied around her curlers, to be presentable at chapel.

It was a household where women wore costumes to do chores in: floral patterned housecoats – which accidentally matched the keep-clean covers put over the good sofa to keep it that way. A place where birth was given in the upstairs room with the doctor in attendance, and although the screams of labour rattled the light fittings, civilised behaviour continued in the kitchen below with *please* and *thank you*, eyes scrunched up to hold in the tears prompted by Mam's roaring above. And despite all that, we were still expected to believe babies were found under cabbage leaves on the allotment, or that my siblings were trafficked in via the doctor's big black medicine bag…

That's how it was in those days: taught to hold two diametrically opposing realities at the one time – a wonderful preparation for deception; to pretend we were in a calm domestic setting whilst the opposite was the case; trained to block out anything that distracted from our sustaining a fictitious parallel illusion.

Or what some people call ACTING.

(3) OUTSIDE THE ACTOR'S STUDIO: THE 'SECRET ARTS' OF THE PERFORMER

On video: An American PRESENTER *sits with index cards in front of him. As a television/internet series, he gives direct address.*

PRESENTER:

So…what is acting? What, precisely, is the 'work' of the actor? And how do actors prepare to play a specific role?

These are just a few of the questions we'll be exploring with you here, in the heart of New York City, 'Outside the Actor's Studio'. Today someone who needs no introduction is with us live to share… The Secret Arts of the Actor.

In costume live on-stage in NATIONAL TREASURE *persona with glasses, scarf and jacket, on live camera:*

NATIONAL TREASURE:

Thank you, Walter, for your kind introduction. Today, I will share with you some sage advice I discovered in my journey as an actor… advice that I have long treasured and still hold dear to both my craft, and my heart. This is the 'advice to actors' offered by the great 18th century French polyglot, encyclopaedist, philosopher and playwright, Denis Diderot in his infamous work, *The Paradox of Acting*. Writing to his contemporaries, Diderot advised the actor to… *(Reads:)*

'Let your body itself expand beyond its surfaces through immediate transformation. Clothe yourself in 'flesh and bone', but beneath that clothing, let not your 'identity be discerned.' Your talent consists *not* in feeling, but in giving a *scrupulous* rendering of the outward *signs* of feeling. Prepare your gestures of despair in a mirror and memorise them! Know the *precise* moment when you will take out your handkerchief (*does so*), and the tears will flow!… That trembling of the limbs, that shaking of the knees, those swoons, those furies: pure imitation…each a lesson learnt in advance… Thus, you, the actor, exaggerates your body, that your body becomes a 'mannequin'… thereby disabling your audience's ability to distinguish your body from your costume…your 'true self' from the character you portray. In this way, the actor's exaggerated body is the actor's body deform'd!!! You have the ability to *choose* to deform, and therefore you can be an 'other', and thereby disappear!'

'That is the quintessential art of the actor.'

(4) STORIES AT NAN'S: SHAKESPEARE

FICTIONALISED AUTOBIOGRAPHY:

Staying at Nan's was being stuck at the turn of
the century – and I'm talking 1901 here, not the
millennium – trapped in a time machine while
the rest of the UK went all groovy and shag-tastic
in that handcart headed straight to hell, or so the
minister assured us. Any dilly-dallying with the
contemporary was not acceptable, and Nan didn't
miss a thing. Like an eagle with a rabbit, she
could spot a copy of *Jackie* a mile and a half away.
And there was no slackening in her strictness,
not even when I was out of hospital but still off
school, recovering from spinal surgery and bored
even more rigid than the hard plastic jacket with
the leather buckles I had to wear. I'd escape
into the front parlour with its parma violets and
solemn tick tock from H Gibson of Pontypridd's
Fusee Dial Clock on the mantelpiece – *tick tock,
tick tock, tick tock* – like a metronome of death.
There wasn't much to read, just the St James
bible, a Reader's Digest *It Shouldn't happen to a
Vet*, the 1956 Hafod Hardware catalogue and
the fat holy tome of the collected works of
Shakespeare. And so into that I would disappear,
like the rabbit finding safety in its hole…

Except there wasn't anything safe about
Shakespeare. It was loud and untrammelled,
full of passion, violence, and sex – and that
was just the comedies. Rape. Murder. Suicide.
Incest: nothing tidy there. And curses. Oh, those
curses…

'Thou elvish-marked, abortive, rooting hog…'

Bloody brilliant.

'…thou lump of foul deformity…
Never hung poison on a fouler toad.
Out of my sight! Thou dost infect my eyes…'

And you couldn't be criticised for being
indulgent, for this was the bard, this was
CULTURE.

(5) HOGARTH'S GARRICK

An image of Hogarth's portrait of Garrick as Richard III appears. She transforms into NATIONAL TREASURE *persona.*

NATIONAL TREASURE:

There! There it is! On the wall! Hogarth's infamous painting of Mr. David Garrick storming the London stage: Drury Lane, 19th October 1741, in Colley Cibber's radical re-shaping of Shakespeare's *Richard III*...

Ever since I started going to the Garrick Club with my fellow actors, I've been mesmerised by this portrait. I'm assuming you do know the Garrick Club – the go-to place for actors in London since 1831...? Well, in case you don't, on the wall is this immense painting – 190.5 centimetres by 250.8 centimetres I believe. Unmissable, really. It depicts the notorious 'tent scene' just before the battle of Bosworth when Richard's conscience pricks and he is haunted by the ghosts of those he's killed...

She uses a laser pointer, directing attention to the parts as audio-described.

In the painting he is starting up from his bed, right hand thrust forward to fend off some phantom adversary, his eyes wild, revealing what is known as, the 'Agitation of Richard's Soul'. At his feet lies his empty armour, a cheerful little memento mori there from Hogarth, foreshadowing defeat and his approaching death – whilst his left hand seizes the sword and so exposes his brutal nature.

Depicted by both Hogarth and Shakespeare, this is indeed a villain, the seducer of widowed Anne not only before the corpse is buried, but scandalously over the actual coffin itself; one happy to dispatch both brother and tender nephews to the next life and seize the throne rather than receive it by divine selection. Further proof of this villainy in Hogarth's portrait comes with Richard literally turning his back on the crucified Christ hanging on the wall behind him – and on his left leg, the garter espousing in Latin his distinguished membership of the heroic and chivalrous Order of the Garter – is distorted to read merely *mal...* Bad. A warning indeed.

After Garrick's electric portrayal, Richard has become one of 'those roles' – a character any serious actor HAS to play.

And every time I've been at the Garrick Club, I think of all the greats who have played him, from Olivier to Cumberbatch… and now, I tremble, as I have been recently approached with the opportunity of possibly being in a potential production maybe sometime in the undisclosed future playing HIM… and I wonder, given the chance, how might I create 'my' Richard – which Richard should I play – and how?

(6) STORIES AT NAN'S: MEMORY

FICTIONALISED AUTOBIOGRAPHY:

I've always had a good memory. Whenever any
of the family were having 'a disagreement' (we
didn't argue, we just 'failed to see eye to eye'), I'd
be fetched, stood on a box, and asked to recall
past conversations word for word like a court
stenographer, to prove who was in the right…

It's a wonderful gift, recall. Such consolation in
hospital on long sleepless nights. Or when you're
in pain. There's nothing better to distract yourself
when being tortured than a good bellow of
iambic pentameter:

'O cursed be the hands that made these holes.
Cursed the heart that had the heart to do it.
Cursed be the blood that let the blood from hence.'

'Poor dwt,' the nurses would say as they stretched
me, tightening the buckles on my surgical brace,
trying to elongate my spine. 'Go on, bach, give it
some welly!' as I yelled out the speeches learnt
by heart.

'If ever [you] have child, abortive be it,
Prodigious, and untimely brought to life,
Whose ugly and unnatural aspect

May fright the hopeful mother at the view
And that be heir to this unhappiness...'

Nobody ever commented on how appropriate, or otherwise, it was for me to be quoting from *Richard III*. They were just some of the many speeches ingrained in my memory during those long Sunday afternoons at Nan's.

But as I grew – and grew crooked, despite the nurses' best efforts – those speeches took on more than a passing significance.

(7) LOOKING FOR RICHARD

On video. NATIONAL TREASURE persona in a red telephone box, on the phone.

NATIONAL TREASURE:

Hello, oh hello, is this Philippa Langely at the Richard III Society…? I'm calling because I'm looking for my Richard. Well, when I say mine, I mean the one I should play in this production… Yes, Richard III… yes, that one. And given that you found the REAL Richard – the historical one, the King, in the car park in Leicester – I was wondering – can you help me find mine?

(8) STORIES AT NAN'S: MILWAUKEE

Image of the Milwaukee brace projected.

FICTIONALISED AUTOBIOGRAPHY:

The Milwaukee brace is also known as a cervico-thoraco-lumbo-sacral orthosis. It consists of a neck ring with a throat mould, two occipital pads, a leather pelvic girdle, aluminium uprights, leather L-shaped thoracic pads and metal bars in the front and in the back. Lateral pads are strapped to these bars and adjustment of these straps holds the spine in alignment.

The Milwaukee brace is used in the treatment of postural disorders or spinal curvature in children who have not reached their growth spurt.

The Milwaukee brace is often prescribed to be worn twenty-three hours a day until the patient reaches skeletal maturity and growth ceases... Or in my case, until lunchtime, when I'd manage to persuade one of the teachers to take it off me, so I could run around the playground like the other boys and girls.

At first I hated wearing it. It was hard and uncomfortable, and I smelt like someone you'd find living rough under a bridge with all the white spirit they put on me to protect my hips and chin from the constant rubbing. Then, after I'd convinced the class I was bionic like *The Six Million Dollar Man* on telly – only better, because I was a ten year old girl and in real life – I started to – not like it exactly – but see it differently…

'It's a badge of honour,' Nan said. 'Sign of your battle wounds. That Milwaukee brace is a symbol of all you've gone through so far.'

Milwaukee… Largest city in the state of Wisconsin USA, Milwaukee.
A lovely word… Milwaukee… From the Native American Algonquian word *Millioke* meaning 'Good', 'Beautiful' and 'Pleasant land'. Good. Beautiful. Pleasant land. Good. Beautiful…

They called me Quasi at school, asked after Esmeralda and queried how the campanology was coming along. Google it. Or do what Nan always said: 'Improve yourself – look it up in the dictionary, twpsyn.' *Camp-pan-ol-o-gy*… That was what constituted bullying from the posh middle-class girl whose parents got *The Telegraph* from London rather than *The Western Telegraph and Pembrokeshire News* which we all read. It didn't bother me, the Quasimodo-ing, because he was gentle and loving, loyal, and in the end the best out of the whole bunch. No, I was quite fond of the old crook-back, and as Lleucu, my best friend, said: 'But you don't ring no bells.' And I didn't.

It was after the 360th anniversary of Shakespeare's birth that things changed… 23rd April… not a day we'd celebrated before, it also being St George's Day… but that year some bright spark at school decided it would be edifying to introduce us to English culture, you know, open up our horizons a little to foreign ways via a special film show. So into the main hall we all trooped, all fifty-seven of us – it was a small school – the lights were switched off and the curtains pulled across the windows to make it dark enough for the huge projector set up in the middle of the aisle. And then everything went monochrome and a man with a fake nose, black Purdey from *The New Avenger's* pageboy wig and slightly padded shoulder strutted into view:

(As Olivier.) 'Now is the winter of our discontent
Made glorious summer by this sun of York;
And all the clouds that lour'd upon our house
In the deep bosom of the ocean buried.
Now are our brows bound with victorious wreaths;
Our bruised arms hung up for monuments;
Our stern alarums chang'd to merry meetings,
Our dreadful marches to delightful measures…'

I knew the speech – it was one I'd learned at Nan's – but I'd never imagined it like this – all sneering, and callous, with those dead, shark eyes – no feeling, no warm blood, just delight at doing evil. And although Olivier's hump wasn't as big as ones I'd come to see later in my life, it was the most meaningful, for it meant wickedness. And suddenly as we sat there in the darkened hall, I felt a shift and my schoolmates started looking at me *differently* – like I was the family pet with too much wolf in me.

Woof. Woof.

(9) LOOKING FOR RICHARD: THE ACTOR'S WORK

NATIONAL TREASURE:

As I've been approached about the possibility of potentially playing Richard III, I join a long tradition of questionable actors who questioned and indeed quested how to play this Everest – no, this Matterhorn of a part. So as part of my research I've been exploring how others have prepared.

Some of you here tonight may be familiar with 'the actor's work' – but just as likely, some of you may *not* be aware of how an actor prepares to play a complex character like Richard III. Take for example Antony Sher and his 1984 performance of Richard for the RSC at Stratford –a performance which ultimately garnered for him both an Olivier and Evening Standard Best Actor award… Sher prepared for the role over twelve months –a process he documents in great detail in his book *(she brandishes it) Year of the King.* As part of his research – the kind many actors undertake in order to 'create' their character, to get 'inside the skin' of who they think this character might be – Tony shows up at Marylebone Medical Library where he explains,

'I'm an actor about to play Richard the Third...
do you have any books on deformities?'

(10) LOOKING FOR RICHARD: IN WARDROBE

On video. NATIONAL TREASURE backstage in a corridor outside Wardrobe Dept.

NATIONAL TREASURE:

I've just been in wardrobe: I'm speechless. I held in my own hands Ian Holm's cloven-hoofed foot, Ian Richardson's withered prosthetic arm and Alan Howard's clown shoe. So ingenious – boots built up to look like club feet and Howard's was spectacular, with studs and a chain to lift and pull the leg along, like a reluctant dog going walkies. Wardrobe mistress dug out some used humps – Sher's custom built 'my deformity' as he called it – and vests with the humps built into them. There were side humps and two lovely central humps recycled for the goblins in panto season. She suggested I try one, but I shrank away. The idea of building my Richard on top of another actor's deformity seems wrong. Worse than that, it seems somehow unhygienic.

(11) A BODY LIKE MINE

PROFESSIONAL ACTOR PERSONA:

As an actor, I've always had to work against type.
A body like mine isn't neutral, it can't sit on the
fence. It's psychological, apparently, the way
my body's seen. People assume because my top
half's twisted, the rest of me must be, too. That
bodies like this belong to blood-thirsty murderers
who have nothing better to do on a Saturday
afternoon between watching the rugby and
putting the kettle on than suffocate their brother's
children.

It's something to do with symmetry. Apparently.
I'm not a perfect rhomboid, a parallelogram, so
I must be sociopathic and not to be trusted with
nephews or other small mammals.

It's unfortunate and wrecks havoc with my
working life. I always wanted to be – not a
household name, but someone you'd pass on the
way to the cold meats counter in the supermarket
who was vaguely familiar. Someone happily
making Equity minimum with repeat fees from
being in the background, nodding and mouthing
*'ribbit rabbit ribbit rabbit ribbit rabbit rhubarb
rhubarb'* over the tea and scones in the caff, or
checking the quality and width of a skirt on the

adjacent market stall, but no, I'm too memorable, apparently. I have a silhouette that lingers long in the memory. And what that silhouette says isn't appropriate for Sunday evening family entertainment.

Apparently.

(12) STORIES AT NAN'S: HUNCHBACK

FICTIONALISED AUTOBIOGRAPHY:

I've never liked the word *hunchback*. Makes me think of someone who can't make their minds up, *(she starts shrugging and hunching shoulders)*, who hasn't an opinion, who doesn't care one way or another about anything. Either that, or a person so timid, so afraid, they spend their life hunched over in dread, waiting for the blow to fall...

'You should never apologise for being who or what you are,' Nan said over the solemn pouring of the tea one afternoon not long after the film show at school. I'd been quiet for a few days, drawing back into myself. 'If you act like you're *dim gwerth rhech dafod,'* she said, putting the cosy back over the pot like she was sheathing the Eucharist, 'then everyone else will treat you like you're *dim gwerth rhech dafod...'* Not worth a sheep's fart.

I'd never considered myself a hunchback. I was *'someone experiencing a disorder of the posture'*, as Nan put it. But after this Richard film at school, there was a change: people looked at me suspiciously, like they weren't quite sure of me, or, worse, like they pitied me – thinking I'd be as unhappy with my body as that Richard was about his, poor dab. How could I feel loathsome, as he did, about this body I so loved? It was my home. It is my home. How could I ever be negative about something like that?

Now it was my turn to be suspicious. There was something not quite right about this Shakespeare Richard…

(13) LOOKING FOR RICHARD

Video of FICTIONALISED AUTOBIOGRAPHY *persona in red phonebox, on the telephone.*

FICTIONALISED AUTOBIOGRAPHY:

Hello, oh hello, is this Philippa Langely at the Richard III Society? I'm calling because I'm looking for my Richard... And given that you found the REAL Richard – the historical one, the king, in the car park in Leicester –I'm wondering can you help me find mine?

(14) LOOKING FOR RICHARD: RESEARCH

NATIONAL TREASURE:

Inspired by Antony Sher's *Year of the King*, I've been keeping, as part of my actorly research, my own journal of observation as I tackle the revelation of true craft through impersonating, like Tony, my exact physical opposite... my own take on the actor's body 'deformed':

I've decided to make the radical decision of exploring Richard as a six-foot four non-disabled rugby player. Following Tony's example, I need to observe unobserved for my research – how do they walk, hold themselves, move? And where do the active non-disabled gather? I ask my friend the chiropodist and she suggests her local rugby club. Like Tony visiting the quote unquote 'spastics clubs', I decide to go undercover, but as a Saint John's ambulance volunteer.

Although they're norm, many of them look quite atypical if I squint, so I proceed, squinting, trying, like Tony, not to show my discomfort. I don't know how to talk to them, I'm not confident about how to interact. I know they're human and in many ways they're like me, but although it gets easier, like for Tony, I still have my panicky moments when one of them looks at me in a really normal way. It's so unfreaky and normative I don't know what to do.

It's not their fault they weren't born like me and it's sobering to think they'll have to wait and hope they develop an impairment later in life. It's humbling; I take so much for granted.

After the game, I feel strangely inspired, uplifted by their courage to be absolutely normal – but then I realise the feeling is just pity and relief I wasn't like them. This isn't the route for me to find my Richard, so I abandon snooping and journaling, for my own sake, if not for the public's, and reluctantly leave the rugby players alone.

(15) STORIES AT NAN'S: SOURCES

FICTIONALISED AUTOBIOGRAPHY:

Being with Nan was a mix of Barbara Woodhouse dog training, except for humans – SIT! – Mary Berry's baking (with half the sugar) – and Patience Strong's homely advice, on steroids. It wasn't always the most comfortable of environments, but it was the place I wanted to be, especially if something was niggling me.

She'd sit at the head of the table, holding her teacup in her hands like it was a chalice, eyeing me over her bifocals:

'If something's bothering you, if something doesn't feel right, if something makes you question, don't be twp, girl, paid bod fel coes brwsh… (Translation: as dull as a broom) *You go and trace it back,'* she'd say, *'like the Amazon, the Orinoco, or our own great Afon Teifi – you follow that back, girl, trace it to its source – and then you'll know… then you'll understand…'*

So, it's taken a while, but that's what I'm doing, going to the sources. Just like those long Sunday afternoons in Nan's front parlour when I was little, I've been reading a lot – but this time, it's the historical Richard rather than Shakespeare's Richard. There's: David Hipson's *Richard III,*

David Horspool's *Richard III: A Ruler and his Reputation,* Annette Carson's *Richard III: The Maligned King,* Philippa Langley and Michael Jones' *The Search for Richard III,* and Susan Fern's book: *The Man Who Killed Richard III.*

And you know what? If the Welsh poet, Guto'r Glyn, is to believed, it was Rhys ap Thomas, born in Llandeilo, who *'killed the boar, shaved his head'* with a fatal blow to Richard's skull with his halberd. Brutal. And that made ap Thomas both a King slayer and a King maker, for that paved the way to the throne for Henry Tudor. And that wasn't the only Welsh connection – and being Welsh, I wanted to find out more – so I took myself off along 'The Henry Tudor trail' – from where Henry landed – in Wales! – to the fatal battlefield at Bosworth, where Richard was killed…

ON THE TUDOR TRAIL: TOWARDS BOSWORTH

Video: FICTIONALISED AUTOBIOGRAPHY *persona, filmed at Cardigan Castle, interacts with her live version.*

FICTIONALISED AUTOBIOGRAPHY (VIDEO):

So…here I am, outside Cardigan Castle, on the 'Henry Tudor trail', following Henry's journey toward Bosworth. He landed just down the road from here at Dale. Are you there?

FICTIONALISED AUTOBIOGRAPHY (LIVE):

Yes, I'm here, ready!

VIDEO:

Are you showing everyone where Dale is located on the map?

LIVE:

Yes! *(She unfurls an old map of Wales and uses a wooden pointer to trace the trail.)* As we were just saying, it was on 7th August, 1485 that Henry Tudor landed at this secluded spot near Milford Haven with his army of 2,000 French mercenaries and those who had been in exile with him, all funded by the King of France.

VIDEO:

But why there?

LIVE:

Well, Henry was born just over here in Pembroke Castle – he was Welsh.

VIDEO:

Never!

LIVE:

Oh yes… His grandfather was one of the Tudors of Penmynydd, Anglesey…from up here.

VIDEO:

No!

LIVE:

Yes! What better place to land than this secluded spot away from Richard's spies and where his Uncle Jasper, Earl of Pembroke, no doubt encouraged him to land. Swelled by the support of Uncle Jasper and some of the local Welsh, Henry then marched with his army to Haverfordwest, here, on his way north.

VIDEO:

So it was here, Cardigan Castle, on August 10th where Henry's ranks swelled after meeting Richard Griffith and John Savage and their followers. Imagine all those *allez les bleus! Allez les bleus!* and Cymros pouring along here on their march north.

LIVE:

Yes. Imagine… Even Rhys Ap Thomas, Richard's main officer in Wales and soon to be his fatal barber, threw his support behind Henry. Not that Richard knew that, not until much later… on the battlefield…

Are you still here? Haven't you more of this Tudor trail to follow?

VIDEO:

You're right. I have. I'm off. Ta'ra.

LIVE:

It was a 200 mile march through Wales to Bosworth for Henry, and soon as he landed he raised the banner of Cadwaladr, the Welsh king from legend.

Video: FICTIONAL AUTOBIOGRAPHY persona appears in rural West Wales, beside a sign for Llanarth.

VIDEO:

Here I am again, on the 'Henry Tudor trail' in Llanarth, said to be one of the oldest settlements in Ceredigion – and where The Llanarth Group is based. According to 'A Topographical Dictionary of Wales, 1833' Henry Tudor *'was hospitably entertained by Einon ap Dafydd Llwyd at Plas Y Wern on his route through this county to*

Bosworth Field' – just over the crossroads behind
me at Gilfachreda. Henry and his swelling ranks
marched right by here, past the village school
behind me – yes, along the A487, yeah, attracting
followers by claiming to be Y Mab Darogan, the
son of prophesy, who would lead the Welsh out
of oppression…

LIVE:

Well, as Nan'd say… They'll promise you
the birds in the bushes, but you'll catch them
yourself…

(16) OUTSIDE THE ACTOR'S STUDIO: MORE 'SECRET ARTS'

On video: American PRESENTER *in interview scenario with* NATIONAL TREASURE *persona.*

PRESENTER:

Hello, and welcome back to 'Outside the Actor's Studio', here in the heart of New York City. Our special guest tonight continues our on-going exploration of the art and craft of the actor, joining the long and distinguished line of award-winning actors who have appeared with us: Dustin Hoffman, Sir Ian McKellen, Robert De Niro, and some of the great Welsh actors including Sir Anthony Hopkins and, of course, Dame Catherine Zeta-Jones. It is my gift and pleasure to introduce the individual who needs no introduction…the inimical, unparalleled, and greatest Welsh actor never to have won a single Bafta, Oscar, Olivier, or any other award… never been given roles she deserved… nor even been auditioned for roles she really should have played. Please welcome her back to Outside the Actor's studio.

NATIONAL TREASURE (LIVE) persona appears live onstage while simultaneously she enters on the video and takes her seat (VIDEO).

VIDEO:

Thank you, Walter.

PRESENTER:

As you know, this evening our purpose is to
get up close and personal…to explore what has
shaped you – the artist and the person who sits in
that chair – so that we can learn about how you
approach your work as an actor.

VIDEO:

Well as an actor, Walter, I've always had to work
against type…

Video continues, but dialogue fades, spoken by LIVE persona:

LIVE:

A body like mine says certain things very loudly,
apparently.
It says Beware…' It says 'Untrustworthy'. It says
'twisted body, twisted mind.'
Apparently.
A body like mine says 'sins of the father' –
punishment from a previous life.
A body like this is always outside the circle.
It says 'mark of the devil.'

It speaks – but not loudly enough to sustain a
career – or so the drama schools told me when
I auditioned. And it wouldn't be fair to give
me false hope – it wouldn't be right to take my
money and offer a place – it wouldn't be ethical
to run me into debt with fees and a student loan
when I'd get no work afterwards.
Apparently.

(17) LOOKING FOR RICHARD: – JCB IN WEST WALES

FICTIONALISED AUTOBIOGRAPHY (VIDEO) persona appears in the cab of a JCB.

FICTIONALISED AUTOBIOGRAPHY (VIDEO):

Well, here I am, looking for my Richard. If Philippa Langley was able to find the REAL Richard – the historical one – the king – in the car park in Leicester, I figured I might do a bit of 'digging' myself here in Wales. And with a bit of rooting around, this is what I've discovered–

Cywydd i'r Brenin Richard a Ddistrywiodd ei Ddau Nai, Meibion Brenin Edward…a poem from 1485 about Richard…in old Welsh!

You see, just after Henry Tudor and his forces killed Richard at Bosworth, the Welsh gentleman and bard, Dafydd Lloyd from Mathafarn just outside Machynlleth, composed one of the first pieces of propaganda against Richard, calling him 'little' – which is not to be confused with the other Little Richard… The bard describes the deceased king as 'a mole', a 'Jew', a 'Saracen', a 'dog', and an 'ape' of 'evil nature' – mild stuff compared to Shakespeare, but it does show us one thing: the Welsh also played a part in creating Shakespeare's monstrous Richard.

(18) LOOKING FOR RICHARD: 'DEFORMITIES'

NATIONAL TREASURE:

As I've been approached about the opportunity of potentially playing Richard III in a production possibly sometime in the future, I've been researching all the different ways my fellow actors have tackled the part in the past. One thing I've discovered is thesps do love a good deformity… So here's a slideshow of some of the more recent celebrated manifestations:

(She uses a pointer to introduce each projected image – close-ups of the paraphernalia used to crip-up, but not showing the faces of the actors, which are pixelated.)

First up: the simple 'I'm clearly not disabled but putting a brace on a leg that is clearly *not* a disabled leg so that I know you know that I'm *not* disabled' look. It's nice, but lacking a little in the warped twistedness so many go for… But Velcro…and the brace seems to be made out of tent pegs – interesting…

This is the somewhat more compelling and arresting 'twisted leg with a transformer-looking brace complete with Bond villain black gloved hand and fashionable but no doubt deadly cane (perhaps with a hidden bayonette)' look…

There's beautiful intricate metal work on this brace. Really quite kinky that.

Ah, now. Here's a variation on the 'drooping hand' look, which takes the withered arm to a whole new level. Far too much unnecessary metalwork for my liking, and that leather strap around the neck… Personally I think it looks like a fan belt.

Oh yes. 'Hunchback play the spider' look. How this Richard ever got on horseback beats me: two crutches, long sleeves, a very large false hump, quite implausible. Nice necklace though…so important for wooing Anne.

And here is the 'post-dramatic visibly strapped-on-hunch with oversized clown shoe so you clomp around like a clumsy idiot' look… I don't think it came with a red-nose, but we could of course try that…

And finally… 'The flash the flesh so everyone knows you aren't really disabled, but are performing naked, clothed merely in a cushion, comedy shoe and your talent' look.

All this ingenuity sent me back to that great 18th century French polyglot, encyclopaedist, philosopher and playwright, Denis Diderot –

who we met earlier this evening, and his infamous work, *The Paradox of Acting*.

(Reads.) 'In this way, the actor's exaggerated body is the actor's body deform'd!! You have the ability to choose to deform, and therefore you can be an-other, and thereby disappear!'

So... have *I* the ability to choose to 'deform'? Can I be an 'other' and thereby disappear??

(19) STORIES AT NAN'S: MOTIVATIONAL SPEAKER

FICTIONALISED AUTOBIOGRAPHY:

I suppose nowadays they'd call Nan a life coach,
or a motivational speaker, if you're the kind to be
encouraged from being insulted in Welsh...
'Don't be *fel rhech mewn pot jam*'– a fart in a jam
jar – she'd say whenever I was disheartened,
glaring at me like a Greek Orthodox religious
icon presiding over the bara brith.

'I don't care what others say you can or cannot
do, girl. *Deuparth gwaith yw ei ddechrau* – starting
the work is two thirds of it – you get going,
twmffat, you look the nay-sayers in the eye and
don't let anyone stand in your way.'

Which is good advice, but hard when you're
four feet three inches and eyeballing someone
means out-staring their beer gut. And it's hard
being gung-ho one rejection after another, being
not-so-gently guided to the sidelines, advised to
take a part less active and more off-stage. And it's
difficult when people treat you differently than the
way they do others, in a perhaps not so equal way.

'...I cannot flatter and look fair,
smile in men's faces, smooth, deceive and cog,
Duck with French nods and apish courtesy...

Cannot a plain man live and think no harm
But thus his simple truth must be abused
With silken, sly, insinuating jacks?'

And suddenly, I found my way back to those
speeches learnt by heart in Nan's front parlour –
and myself on the battlefield at Bosworth, the end
of the Tudor trail, questioning the treatment of
historical Richard.

VIDEO – BATTLE OF BOSWORTH RE-ENACTMENT MONTAGE

And I stood there with the re-enactment going
on all around me, dressed as I was for battle,
thinking of the warrior with scoliosis like mine,
the successful soldier and accomplished leader
of men. And I thought of the popular ruler who
reformed in favour of the poor, whose rights
to the throne were beyond question, who died
protecting the realm from a coup, a man who had
recently lost both wife and heir. And I thought
of how the events in Shakespeare's play didn't
match the known facts, how the body in the
car park in Leicester lacked the withered arm,
dragging leg, cloven foot, stone heart. And I
thought of the less legitimate Henry Tudor, and of
the years of the War of the Roses and a country
tired of fighting. And I thought how powerful
propaganda might be, how a reputation could
be sullied, how a drama could demonise a once
hero, how physical difference could be made
fearful in the skilled playwright's hand, writing to
please powerful patrons.

(20) OUTSIDE THE ACTOR'S STUDIO: 'THE PRIVATE MOMENT'

On video, American PRESENTER, as before.

PRESENTER:

Welcome back to Outside the Actor's Studio. In a
unique development, this evening's special guest
has agreed to allow us a glimpse of part of her
process as she prepares to consider the possibility
of taking on the role of Richard III, should it
ever be offered. She is participating in the most
celebrated/iconic exercise we have developed
here, Outside the Actor's Studio: 'the private
moment'.

*The following becomes a live voiceover on microphone, while
SERIOUS ACTOR persona appears onstage. Contrary to the
descriptions, she stands stock still, staring at the audience.*

As you can see, our special guest is beginning her
work. You may not be able to hear her, but she
is muttering, over and over again, 'Jesus Christ!
Jesus Christ!' She has begun to wave her arms,
releasing various cries and gasps, ohs and ahs. We
all begin to steal a glimpse of this private moment
of preparation, and it is an absolutely charming
and delightful moment… She is completely
oblivious to our presence as she stays focused,

moving to sensory work on a variety of imaginary objects. She strokes the air, makes circles with her hands and now rectangles. The lights are shifting. I announce: 'A scene from *richard III redux'*. Uninterrupted by my announcement, she stays absolutely focused within this private moment. Lights on or off, it clearly makes no difference because she is fully 'in the zone'. And me, how do I feel? I feel like I am observing an absolutely private scene that is *none of my business*, and I suspect this is precisely what we are all supposed to feel. This is NOT a character she is putting on, but it *is HER*…the private individual, revealed before you, now.

(21) A BODY LIKE MINE

SERIOUS ACTOR:

A body like mine can't play the doctor. A body
like mine can't play the love interest. A body like
mine can't play the detective, the news anchor,
the master chef, the hero. A body like this can't be
a parent, the boss, a gunslinger; it can't drive the
getaway car, carry the bomb, or be a double agent.
A body like this doesn't feature in love scenes.
It can't be Juliet to someone else's Romeo.

NATIONAL TREASURE:

A body like mine can't play the Principle Boy.
A body like mine can't play the prima donna.
A body like mine can't play the CEO, the
pathologist, the girl next door, the heart throb. A
body like this can't be the expert, the crinolined
lady, the scullery maid. It can't deliver babies,
solve a crime, be prime minister, belt out tunes.
A body like this doesn't feature in love scenes.
It can't be Juliet to someone else's Romeo.

FICTIONALISED AUTOBIOGRAPHY:

A body like mine can't play the doctor. A body
like mine can't play the love interest. A body like
mine can't play the detective, the news anchor,
the master chef, the hero. A body like this can't be

a parent, the boss, a gunslinger; it can't drive the
getaway car, carry the bomb, or be a double agent.
A body like this doesn't feature in love scenes.
It can't be Juliet to someone else's Romeo.

SERIOUS ACTOR:

A body like mine can't play a body like mine.
A body like this can't play Richard.

She puts on the chainmail hood.

(22) WHAT SEE YOU HERE, NOW?

Echo of the opening. Performed live, SERIOUS ACTOR, *against video montage of moody b/w castle footage.*

SERIOUS ACTOR

What see you here, now, before you?
Yes, I am both a dissembler…an ac-tor…
And the thing-itself.

So how does one ready-made
'deform'd, unfinish'd…
scarce half made up'
take on and play my self-same form?

Am I not holy whole, even in my mis-shapen
form?

And on the 'morrow when you wake
how will you remember me?
As one 'deform'd, unfinish'd'
that stood before you on *this* stage,
Or as the one who re-makes your re-membrance.
I, who would never re-shape my form,
nor transform this self-same shape,
On the 'morrow who will I be for you?

To be, or not to be Richard, that is *still*
my question.

AND SUDDENLY I DISAPPEAR…
THE SINGAPORE/UK 'd' MONOLOGUES

CONTEXT

In 2016 lead Singapore collaborator Peter Sau and I began talking of this project, with a desire for international dialogue around diversity, disability, and what it is to be human. Peter was extremely interested in the long history of professional Deaf and disabled-led art in the UK, a product of our Disabled People's Movement. He and his growing team of collaborators were keen to learn of models and approaches from the UK experience which might be useful during Singapore's own individual journey towards Disability arts (as opposed to arts and disability, which is often led by the non-disabled for 'the disabled'). I shared the process I had developed since 2009 with the initiation of *The 'd' Monologues* project and we agreed this would be a good model for the first multilingual, intercultural Deaf and disabled-led project between Singapore and the UK. We began applying for funding, and I was fortunate to be awarded an Unlimited International Commission and so the process began.

Peter gathered an extraordinary team of allies, researchers, translators and transcribers, and a vast number of Deaf and disabled interviewees willing to share their stories, knowing these previously unreported narratives would inspire my fictional monologues. I am grateful to the many who have participated, and the excellent team members who have worked with such diligence, sensitivity and care on all aspects of the project.

I was impressed by the energy, generosity, persistence and pure *joie de vivre* of D/deaf and disabled Singaporeans, who revealed a familiar emotion to the interviews I led in the UK – the frustration of being made invisible. *And Suddenly I Disappear* honours the many opinions, beliefs, and experiences of disabled and D/deaf people in Singapore and beyond – but it is a work of the imagination, informed by my own aesthetics and politics, and any errors or deficiencies are mine alone.

In this brief discussion, I cannot do justice to the astonishing integrity and dedication shown by my Singapore collaborators and all those who participated in this 'game-changing' project. It is to all these remarkable individuals – too many to mention by name – that these fictional texts are dedicated.

And Suddenly I Disappear: The Singapore/UK 'd' Monologues was commissioned and supported by Unlimited, celebrating the work of disabled artists, with funding from Arts Council Wales and British Council. Its world premiere was at Gallery Theatre, National Museums Singapore, 25 May 2018, produced by Access Path Productions. Its UK premiere, with new monologues and guest performers, opened The Unlimited Festival, Southbank Centre, London, 5th September 2018, produced by The Llanarth Group.

Credits for the World premiere of *The Singapore 'd' Monologues* at The Gallery Theatre, National Museums Singapore, produced by Access Path Productions:

Director & Executive Producer	Phillip Zarrilli
Associate Director & Performer	Peter Sau
Visual Language Director	
& Performer	Ramesh Meyyappan
Producer & Performer	Grace Khoo
Co-Sound Designer	
& Performer	Danial Bawthan
Performers	Sara Beer
	Stephanie Esther Fam
	Agnes Lim
	Lee Lee Lim
	Sophie Stone (Video)
Associate Producer	Natalie Lim
Lighting Designer	Dorothy Png
Co-Sound Designer	Bani Haykal
Videographer (Singapore)	James Khoo
Videographer (UK)	Paul Whittaker
Production Stage Manager	Stella Cheung
Assistant Production Stage Manager	Abel Koh

Creative Captioner & Operator	Nur Shafiza (Shai)
Marketing Designer	Su Yuen Ho
Lighting Operator	Huang Xiangbin
Technical Crew	Ben Ong, Aaron Cheang, Fiona Lim
Access Support	Shirley Tan
Sign Language Interpreters	Evelyn Chye, Teo Zhi Xiong, Amirah Osman, Nix Sang

The UK premiere *The Singapore/UK 'd' Monologues* at Unlimited Festival, Southbank Centre, London, 5th September 2018, produced by The Llanarth Group:

Director & Executive Producer	Phillip Zarrilli
Visual Language Director & Performer	Ramesh Meyyappan
Associate Producer	Natalie Lim
Producer & Performer	Grace Khoo
Performers	Peter Sau
	Sara Beer
	Danial Bawthan (Video)
	Stephanie Esther Fam (Video)
	Lee Lee Lim (Video)
	Sophie Stone (Video)
	Garry Robson
	Macsen McKay
Stage Management	Katie Bingham
Translators	Peter Sau
	Grace Khoo
	Chim Keng Hoong
	Macsen McKay

BE A RIVER

Be a river. The river does not stop. It finds its way. It carves through stone, through rock, it always finds a way to flow on. At times it is a trickle, at others, wide and broad and it is never-ending and it will not stop.

Be like water. Be like a river. You dip a bowl into the river and the river fills it and becomes the bowl. Pour into a pot, it becomes the pot. Treat with fire and it becomes steam. It becomes soup.

This is how you will be. Unstoppable. Fluid. Powerful. Malleable but independent, following your own route, your own way from source until you reach and merge with the sea.

CAN'T DO

The list of 'can't do' is very long.

It's intimidating and quite humbling, actually.

It's so long I'm not even going to start it, except…
sometimes it's good to face your limitations – not
to be in denial about your life and capabilities,
but to *keep it real.* It's what they focus on in
newspapers and on television – what we *can't* do.
It stops us from living in la-la land, fantasy, and
being just like everybody else. It's a – perhaps
necessary – reminder of the true shape of the
world: just as there's poverty and super-wealth,
there are those who can, and are able. And those
who – well… Those of us who can't.

And I can't do many things.

I can't do logarithms – I tried, at school, but…
I just couldn't see a point in the future when I
would need to assume that *x, y, a,* and *b* are all
positive, that the logarithm quotient rule $log_b(x / y) = log_b(x) - log_b(y)$ should apply to anything, that
the logarithmic function $y = log_b(x)$ is the inverse
function of the exponential function $x = b^y$. And
don't get me started on natural logarithms. When
we were young and innocent at Sunday school,
we thought it was a form of family planning the
Pope approved of.

Filo pastry. There's another. I can't make filo pastry so, I'm sorry, I just buy it frozen, ready – made, and – nobody notices the difference… There! I've said it.

And Chihuahua. I know, but I just can't do yappy little lapdogs, especially when they're carried in handbags or perch shivering in that deeply distressing way in the front basket of a bicycle. It's distracting when I'm driving, and I'm terrified one day I'll run them down in my BMW, or be faced with having to pet one. They're just rats with shorter tails. Why can't people go for a Great Dane or Saint Bernard, an Irish wolfhound, you know, a dog that'll save you from banshees and Vikings and dig you out of avalanches, a beast you can ride and do dressage with, not step on, and have to smear off your shoe?

And New Year. I can't do that *Auld Lang Syne* stuff. *(Sings.)* 'Should old acquaintance be forgot…' Well if they're not with you, either in person, heart, or mind, they clearly weren't that important or close to you to begin with, so – move on. Life is short. Give your energies and blessings at New Year to those who really matter.

And there are so many other can't dos.

I can't play games – I mean mental, mind games,
when people try to manipulate or mess each
other up with this awful power play. I like people,
I don't want to psychologically scar someone, so I
cannot participate in a warped power struggle of
lies and uncertainties.

And I can't do macramé, or basket weaving –
which always surprises people, because they
often think that's what we do: Sit in sheltered day
centres doing crafts – which, actually, I'd love to,
but I'm too busy running a company, raising two
kids and keeping my lover satisfied for that.

And apologetic. I can't be sorry for who I am and
how I look and how that makes you feel – that's
your problem – but I can be sympathetic, and
I can help you overcome your limitations and
expectations of who you think we are and what
we can do. I'm trained. I'm an expert. Trust me.
You're in safe hands.

HOW MANY OHS…?

Oh it's such a shame…

Oh, you're so young.

Oh, they let you out by yourself do they?

Oh I'm so so sorry.

Oh! You didn't want to cross the road?

Oh you're such an inspiration!

Oh…you're not as I expected.

Oh I think you'll find we're really quite tolerant here.

Oh… Baik pe. Sial lah…[1] I didn't expect that…

Oh! You have a job?!

Oh aren't you amazing, considering…?

Oh! You can do that?

Oh – you're really intelligent!

Oh! You have a girlfriend?

Oh I've never really spoken to someone who is, you know… like you, before.

---

1   Wow. Are you for real?

Oh! You have a husband and children!?

Oh bless you. You will be in my prayers.

Oh… you are proud to identify as disabled??!!

Oh! You are not selling tissues, auntie?

Oh, you're amazing!

Oh please – don't come too close.

Oh you are unique, one in a million.

Oh, you cannot be out alone, so where is the person in charge of you?

Oh – are you sure you're not contagious?

Oh… I wish there were others like you…

HONG TOU JIN 红头巾[2]

My grandmother's sister, my great aunt, was sent from Guangdong Province to Singapore with a cardboard suitcase holding rice for the journey, a photograph of the family she was supporting, and her red cloth hat and blue samfoo uniform… She was a Samsui – cheap labour – in the British time, after the war. The Aliens Ordinance had capped the number of Chinese male immigrants, so they started sending women away to work – women who may not have chosen to go, but who knew their duty, and did it.

Carting bricks for forty cents a day, my great aunt embraced frugal spinsterhood, living simply, four to a room, sending whatever they could to the family back home. Or so the official story goes, the one we Singaporeans all know.

My great aunt lived in one of the shop-houses along Eu Tong Sen – Chinatown – sleeping in a hammock and whiling away the evenings in the five foot way. I like to think she kept her red cap starched and bright – a lucky colour to make her distinctive and help avoid the many accidents that were common on construction sites. It was

---

2   Red headscarf.

dangerous work, and lonely, far away from the
ancestral home she was keeping alive, a place
she would never see again, except perhaps in her
sleep.

The sturdiest and most plain were sent, the
ones less likely to find a husband and provoke
heartache from being ruined. Or so my
grandmother said, unapologetic that she was
beauty of the family, making a good match
and bringing if not money, then luck, and the
prospect of good fortune to the family house.

Toiling like a snail on the construction sites, my
great aunt became so bent from carrying bricks
her bones relearnt their shape and became
hunched, doubled over – a permanent physical
impairment – no longer able to unbend. Her
posture reflected her lowly station, unable to
straighten and look others in the eye. A lifetime
scouring the ground.

'Do not pity me,' she said.

你千期唔好可怜我。虽然我头耷耷，係氹水到，係条河
面到，我仲睇到蓝天，仲睇到白云。有时仲有金执添。[3]

---

3   Do not pity me – so much is dropped or thrown away. I have had more
fortune with eyes downcast and I can still see the sky and the clouds in the
river, or puddles as I hurry by.

Or at least this is what I tell myself, creating defiant words for a woman I never knew, but whose genes I share. She did not pity herself, nor would she take others' pity. She was proud of her achievements, my grandmother said, proud of the resilience of her damaged body that sustained the family back home.

佢又殘又廢 – heoi yau can yau fei – damaged and useless.

No. She is my touchstone, one of the disabled ancestors our city is built on, thousands upon thousands, scar upon scar.

AND SUDDENLY I DISAPPEAR 1

And suddenly I disappear. My flesh dissolves and
I'm nowhere –
just a huddle of clothes overlooked on the street.
I'm suddenly not here – a blink and I'm gone
– vanished – erased by your not looking, your
I-see-you-but-I-don't-see-you eyes.
You're a good person. You pay your taxes,
recycle, donate to charity, you pick up your dog's
mess when you walk it in the park. You're kind.
Responsible. You live in a caring society that
values uniformity. Difference is disconcerting.
You do not permit this to exist in your
neighbourhood.
Do I offend you?
Does my presence affect your sense of balance?
My being here contradicts all that you think you
are. So you dissolve me. You strike me through
like a bad sum, the wrong answer. You look
straight through me and I'm not even here.

TAXI DRIVER KARMA

What kind of person steals from the blind? The
Taxi driver refused to accept the note I had given
him was ten dollars.
'Where got? No lah, only five dollar. You blind.
You got guide dog can see, can count for you,
meh?'
Every day I meet people who think they are
comedians…
'I know what I gave you', I said, 'because of the
braille dots on the top right side of the notes.' I'm
proud of our accessible Singaporean dollars.
'No, maybe you siao,[4] your brain up there also
something wrong. Maybe you are not just blind?
Maybe your finger got magic power. Special one
too? Can feel things not there?'
 'You're just not trying,' I said, 'feel again.'
But he swore he couldn't and only gave me
change from a five. What could I do? He taxi
driver. He could drive away fast with me still in.
So it bothers me – was he bad, stealing from the
vulnerable, or had the dots got used up? They
fade with handling and perhaps it takes a tutored
hand – a seeing fingertip, like mine – to notice.

---

4   Crazy.

'Bad luck to him, he will end up punished in hell,' my mother said. 'Maybe he come back blind in the next life, to teach him a lesson.'

And I said 'mother, do you think that's what happened to me? That I'm being punished for something, it's my karma?

But she wouldn't answer.

She wouldn't answer.

ELABORATIONS ON 残

(Definitions as found from Pin Pin Chinese English Dictionary.)

残忍　can ren – cruel

残酷　can ku – cruelty

残暴　can bao – atrocity

残杀　can sha – to slaughter

残毒　can du – vicious

残害　can hai – to devastate

残废　can fei – handicapped

残疾　can ji – deformed and sick

残缺　can que – shattered, incomplete

残骸　can hai – wreckage

残局　can ju – a hopeless situation

残敌　can di – defeated enemy

残渣　can zha – rubbish, debris

残羹　can geng – leftovers

残月　can yue – waning moon

残丘　can qiu – a lone hill

残余　can yu – remnant

残存　can cun – barely surviving

残破　can po – torn and broken

残留　can liu – left behind

IN A ROW...

1 Her grandparents said they were cursed, which was why she was born as she was.

2 Neighbours didn't give congratulations cards, as they had on the births of the other children.

3 *(Sign language.)* They were so happy! Their baby was going to be just like them. Who wanted a baby with a different way of communicating, experiencing, being? Hearing was all very well, they supposed, but it wasn't for them.

4 It happened suddenly. People said it was 'tragic' and 'unlucky'.

5 In the end, he said nothing mattered except they were together and happy. Anything else was just detail.

1 An aunt came to take her away. They said it would be better for everyone – including her – in the long run.

2 It wasn't that they were commiserating, they just didn't know what to say. Did you still smile and say well done, I'm happy for you, if the parents ended up with someone they hadn't expected?

3 *(Sign language.)* To celebrate this new arrival, they invited all the family around for a feast.

4 Everything was difficult at first, but nothing she couldn't handle.

3 *(Sign language.)* They were still celebrating at midnight, but the neighbours put up with the noise, too happy for the new family to complain.

2 They worried he'd be bullied at school. Would the other children accept him, or reject him for not being like them?

1 The aunt told them to forget her, to wipe clean the slate, pretend she had never been, to try again, for a 'normal' child.

3 *(Sign language.)* They were so happy with their baby – so quick to learn, so visual, so funny.

1 But her mother could not forget.

4 It was funny – accessible toilets with steps! She had to laugh.

2 They hated the term 'special' – wasn't everyone special?

4 A sense of humour was essential – and patience, and energy. Change would come. She started campaigns for access and equality.

1 Her mother could not forget, nor wipe clean
   the slate, nor abandon her own flesh and blood,
   although she did send the aunt away. Dealing
   with the doctor was more difficult, but she
   persisted. This was her child.

5 Life was all about change and learning new
   things, he decided, and adapting to the
   circumstances they found themselves in.

1 Her child.

2 And this phrase: 'Special needs'… Everyone is
   special – and doesn't everyone have needs?

5 It was about growth and evolution. And he was
   evolving, and they were both moving forwards to
   what was becoming a better frame.

3 *(Sign language.)* So fast with learning to sign – and
   lip-reading English, too. So clever! Bilingual
   already!

5 At kindergarten the other children just embraced
   a new friend to play with. It was their parents
   who shuddered and taught their watchful children
   difference.

BLIND CAT VISION

Children's schoolyard chant in Mandarin:

瞎眼猫, 瞎眼猫
看你的本领高不高

瞎眼猫, 瞎眼猫
看你的本领高不高

瞎眼猫, 瞎眼猫
看你的本领高不高[5]

Three blind mice, three blind mice,
See how they run, see how they run,
They all run after the farmer's wife
Who cuts off their tails with a carving knife,
Have you ever seen such a thing in your life
As three blind mice, three blind mice.

We rely too much on surface, what we see with
our eyes.
Now I laugh when people pull their children
away from me on public transport, like blindness
is catching. I'm not contagious. I will not infect.
I know they don't *mean* to hurt me… Life has
taught me to be generous and patient. Look at
me: I am someone with real vision.

---

5   Blind cat, blind cat / What you can do…?

NON-BELIEVER

I don't believe in disability – I mean, yes, the
poor sods stuck in bed with lolling heads that
need everything done for them, yeah, sure, it's
clear they're fucked – but some of them, you
know, dancing around at charity gigs, doing
five-kilometre sponsored walks for lesbian dogs,
wanking off about prejudice and whatever with
their 'see the person not the condition' – them
– I go: Yeah, I see you alright…I can see there's
nothing the fuck wrong with you, mate, with
your online petitions for equality in swimming
pools and jobs for the disadvantaged and
underprivileged – that's just another word for crap
– they're not discriminated against, they're just
shit. If they had any real balls and talent, they'd
be fine, like that scrunched-up bloke in the talking
wheelchair – Steven whatsit until he kicked the
bucket – he looked fucked, but he managed. And
managed all over the bloody world.
I hate them do-gooders, those spouting about
needing to include people and be understanding.
I understand. You're fitter than me, yet there
you are, looking for hand-outs. Lazy gits. Can't
even be consistent. This girl at work, right,
she's walking all fine in her clicketty clack shoes

one day, then limping the next, then she's on a
fucking zimmer frame the next week, then back
in her high heels and then fuck me if she isn't
hobbling along on two crutches the week after.
I'm like 'make your bloody mind up, girl' and
she's 'no – it's my disability, it isn't consistent'
and I go 'yeah, right. I can see how you are –
you're fine' – and she goes 'no, I've an invisible
disability' and I go 'look, love, I've seen the signs
– the international symbol for disability, right,
is a wheelchair with a head on it. So disabled is
stuck in a wheelchair – that's what a disabled is
and that's what a disabled looks like – the whole
bloody world's agreed on that, and when you
think how impossible it is to get people around
the world to agree on anything, then you know it
must be right, right?'
Lazy fuckers.
We used to be great – a nation of grafters – didn't
matter that your granddad had emphysema, he'd
still be down that pit, coughing his guts up as
he shovelled away at the coal face for fourteen
hours a day, eleven years of age and already
more of a man than those scroungers will ever be.
Commitment, that's what it was – commitment to
getting the job done, not complaining of having
unions and rights and all that namby pamby

nonsense, just bloody getting on with it, standing on your own two feet. *Independence.* That's what built the empire. Workers with dignity, not scroungers money-grabbing what they can because oooh, their poor sore back, or aaaah, they're a bit blue and can't get out of bed in the morning. That's not depression, that's a lie-in. Bring back the poorhouses, then we'll see how hard-off they are. Like that bloke down the road, lost his legs in a car accident and then said he couldn't go back to work because they didn't have ramps or a lift. It's an old building, listed, what does he expect? Just get himself up the stairs on his arse – that's what my gran did when the tumour pressed on her spine, dragged herself up those stairs every night and back down again in the morning rather than making a bed downstairs and being seen as an invalid. She wasn't a disabled. Too proud to be one of them. And that's what we need again, now. Proper values, none of this spoon-feeding nanny state. People get back to work fast enough when there's no hand-outs they can pad their useless arses with. You have to be cruel to be kind. And I'll smash your fucking face in if you tell me otherwise.

THIS BODY… THAT BODY – EVERYBODY…

… the corpuscles and lymph, the bloody matter,
the meat and muscle, jelly and bone, the skin
and hair, heart and the spleen, the kidneys and
lungs, colon and pancreas, a football pitch of skin,
an eight pint vat of blood, twenty feet of small
intestine, nine metres of the alimentary canal, one
hundred thousand miles of veins, arteries, and
capillaries, a circulatory system that wraps twice
round the earth, one hundred billion neurons,
one spoonful of an eye, cupped hands of one
heart.
The weights and measures, hoists and petards,
bellows and pumps, veins and valves.

This body…That body – everybody…punctures,
bleeds, breaks, fractures.
They detain, disappoint, distil, delight, detonate,
they dance, get disease, decline, decrease,
disintegrate,
they die, decompose, disperse, demonstrate,
demote, demur, demoralise, dement, they
denigrate,
defie, defect, defer, default, they dehydrate,
they deifie, delay, depart, depend, depreciate,
deploy, deplume, deprave, deprive, depopulate
(desires, deserts, desists, detains, it dominates).

They detach.

They despatch.

They dissolve.

This body…

This body is dangerous.

It desires, it delights, it delivers, it dances.

SMILE

One of the biggest changes is I no longer smile.
It's no longer natural, a triggered response.
To smile is an effort.

Smiling is an echo chamber, a call and response.
If no echo, no trigger, it is just a grimace, a baring
of the teeth. To smile is to be human. I will not
lose my humanity. I will practise smiling. I will
do it in the dark, alone, in moments when I'm
not sure anyone is receiving it, perhaps just the
shadows, or the spider with its eight eyes in a web
in the corner of the room, no matter. I will make
myself smile until it becomes second nature.

《笑》(SMILE – MANDARIN TRANSLATION)

其中一个最大的转变是我不再笑了。缺少了外在刺激，这个动作已经不再自然。

笑是一种付出。它犹如一个回音室，有声音就有反应。如果没有了回响和联系，就只是个露出牙齿，面部扭曲的表情。

笑是人类的一种行为，我绝不允许自己丧失人性。我会练习笑。在黑暗里，在孤独中，在不知是否有人会接纳的时候。也许有影子，有蜘蛛在房间里的角落头里织了网，用八只眼睛看着我。

无论如何，我会使我自己笑，持续进行，直到习以为常。

WHAT NOT TO SAY TO SOMEONE WHO IS DEPRESSED

Cheer up, love, it may never happen.
What have you got to be depressed about?
Smile! Look on the bright side.
Just be more positive.
Have you tried being more upbeat?
Why do you have to be so gloomy?
Happiness isn't a given, it's a skill.
You have to work at it. You need to try harder.
Change your diet.
Change your attitude.
Change your life!
Stop being so negative.
No one likes a moody person.
Can't you just be happier? Smile!

I tell you ah these days everyone is damn
pampered.
Everyone is depressed.
You just think of people worse than you, lor.
Poor people hor cannot be depressed.
至少你不是无家可归[6]
至少你没有生在打战的国家[7]
至少你有家人支持你[8]

---

6   At least you're not homeless.

7   At least you're not born in a war zone.

8   At least you have the support of your family.

Eh just pull your socks up lah. It's all in your mind can. You just take bus to Bishan Park and walk walk around. Go and smell the trees. Be uh one with nature. Some more free one leh. Smile and the world smile with you.

SOAP

It was an experiment. I was to be studied. The
actor would shadow me for a week so he could
play a disabled character in his next role.

'What is his condition?' I asked the researcher.
'Is it someone with a sensory or physical
impairment?'

'Yes' the researcher said.

'Is it an intellectual disability, or something like
muscular dystrophy?'

'That's right' the researcher said.

'But if you want to be impairment-specific, if you
want to educate the audience instead of repeating
the same old lies and misconceptions, you need
to be clear about what it is.'

'All of that,' she said. 'All of the above, great,
thanks for accepting.'

So it was set-up and he arrived late on the first
morning.

'Sorry,' he smiled, all teeth and sunglasses.

'Where do we begin?'

'To the MRT[9], now,' I said, 'you've made me late
for work.'

---

1   MRT – Mass Rapid Transport, the Underground train system in Singapore.

'Work? Oh, right, box-packing, something empowering like that, the dignity of manual labour? Wow.'

I find nothing empowering about being treated like a slave, paid a pittance, well below the going rate for being patronised, told how marvellous I am for completing such brain-numbing, menial work.

'No, at the school. We'll miss assembly.'

'You go to school? Wow, that's really progressive.'

'No – ' I was already irritated by the idiot – 'I'm the head of the music department.'

We were delayed further on the MRT, people recognising him and asking for an autograph. Same at the school, the kids double-taking in the corridor and I don't think it was because I slapped him when he tried to help me along the corridors I knew like the back of my hand. He insisted on wearing dark glasses indoors.

'Must you?' I asked. 'Why the shades? It doesn't make you incognito.'

'It's so I know how it is to be vision-impaired, in case we decide that's another challenge the character has to overcome,' he said. 'We don't really know who he is, yet, not his backstory, and I'm lucky, the soap allows me to have a say in his development.'

'But won't that become a chore for you, if you stay in the soap long?' I asked.

'No, he'll just be miraculously cured,' he said, 'or overcome his burden so after a few months we can drop that aspect and the audience will forget.'

'But this is supposed to be a ground-breaking definitive moment of inclusion and diversity,' I said, quoting the text that had made me agree to help in the first place. 'It's supposed to be realistic, reflecting the experience of disabled people in Singaporean society.' I said.

'Yeah,' he said, 'but y'know, the novelty'll wear off after a while, unless we can keep having medical dramas and emergencies to keep the audience interested.'

'But the character was supposed to be just like any other Singaporean,' I said, 'married or divorced, working, with children, blended families, that sort of thing.'

'Woah!' he said. 'I love your vision and that's radical and definitely the way to go, but let's just get them used to a real disabled body on screen first.'

'But you're not,' I said. 'You're not disabled.'

He rolled his eyes.

'That's why it's called acting, man.'

'So why can't a disabled actor play it?'

'You trying to do me out of a job and an award?'

He grinned. 'And anyway, everyone knows there's no disabled actors in Singapore.'

'Just as there's no disabled teachers, or writers, or directors, or shop assistants,' I said, showing him to the door.

'Wow. Disabled actors and directors and writers and doctors and soldiers and buskers and mothers and everything… You're really radical, but not really living in the real world are you, yeah?'

Yeah. Yeah.

NO ONE OWE SINGAPORE A LIVING

I remember the heat of the sunshine in the school yard, lined up like little army platoons, straight backs, standing to attention, and the sunrays pricking at my skin like tiny needles. We were singing *Majulah Singapura* after the flag raising ceremony, facing the principal at the top of the yard. Behind him there was a banner which I would stare at, which we would all stare at, so its message became tattooed with memory at the back of our minds: No one owe Singapore a living. No one owe us a living…?

I was eight. I didn't know what that meant. It was one of our National Education slogans: No one owe us a living… There was something stark about the phrase, chilly – icy blue, exposed. It was only later I realised it had to do with our strong work ethic ingrained from birth, our vitality and independence, the stamina to forge ahead, make a world class city from the chaos of squatters in kampongs, skyscrapers where there was once swamps… It's a cliché, this romantic narrative we've made for ourselves, but it *is* remarkable when you think of what we've achieved in such a short time, what we are – this hodge-podge, this rojak, this rattlebag of assorted

cultures and heritages, languages and gods – our
slogans of harmony, diversity and mutual respect
– our complete strangeness – and yet that isn't
embraced, the rainbow becomes vanilla, we seek
blandness, uniformity – peace. We don't want
racial riots like in 1964, we don't want Chinese
to think as Chinese, the Malay to think as Malay,
Indian as Indian – we want all to think as 'one
people, one nation, one Singapore.' But it is
kiasuism, a fearful competitive mind in pursuit of
the five C's: cash, car, credit card, condominium,
country club membership… and all part of a
monetary machine where we're valued for our
usefulness as impersonal cogs helping the great
wheels of commerce turn… Sometimes there is
a rigidity about what form the cogs must take
– they need to be upright on two limbs, and
move in a certain way, and although it's just as
efficient to roll on four wheels, this doesn't fit the
template, so it is discarded, of no value, no use…
Or so I think…
I've had lots of time to think – many hours
waiting between hospital appointments, brain
endlessly circling on *kia*. Fear.
To distract myself, I think of that schoolyard
and the bannered slogans and the sun pouring
down… and standing, the miracle of just *standing*

in my crocodile line, dressed like a little soldier, sniggering at the girl on crutches before me swaying, determined to stand with the rest of us singing *Majulah Singapura*, but tiring, and shaking and the teacher coming over, telling her 'give up, lah', and still she stood, sweat wet on her face, the effort of just standing... The effort of trying not to flinch as we called her demeaning names 'in fun' to 'include her', the effort of trying to smile and not mind as she was left to the side, yet again, during PE, the effort of trying to hold her head up despite the whispers and patronising smiles from the parents at the school gates who showed her their teeth and never wanted her to associate with their children – with me.

The effort...The effort... No wonder she gave up. If she'd been from a certain part of India the sub-continent and not Little India district, she might have been a goddess – Lakshmi – or an avatar of Ganesh, the remover of obstacles. Her condition might have been considered auspicious, a blessing, something that made her stand out and apart in a good way, as difference is valued. What she had was something extra. She would not be an embarrassment, something to be hidden away because of shame.

Or so I think...

I've been thinking a lot in my many hours
adapting to the new reality, the days trying to
absorb the future… I was not born this way.
I am evolving.
Even though your parents love you, they are the
product of their upbringing and it wasn't so long
ago when aunties came to take away the difficult
new-borns – the ones who suddenly disappeared as
though never were – those who were spirited away
to a convent, a kind orphanage the stories went,
but a path into the jungle might be more truthful.
'It's better this way. She already 'pai liao',[10] so 'pai
mia'.[11] Why make her suffer more? You put dogs out
of their misery, tio boh?[12] Like that, hor, no sense,
no feeling.'
Misshapen cogs cannot be put to work.
Misshapen cogs get sent to the scrapheap,
misshapen cogs are melted down, got rid of, put
aside, for it is easier to keep the machine running
as it always has than wonder if it can work with
slightly different components.
To distract myself, I think back to the school quad,
but it is not a distraction, it is new knowledge.
No one owe us a living…

---

10 Spoilt, damaged.

11 Living a life of misery.

12 Don't you agree?

We would work, and we want to, given the opportunity…

No one owe us a living… but perhaps we are owed a chance.

CURE

1 Not forever, no. If God decides… I have met
   people very ill, bad cancer, legs stop working,
   stroke, doctors give up, say done already, finish,
   go home, die – these people, all restored –
   through power of faith. I have seen them, shook
   their hand. Is possible, can. The Bible is full of
   healing. It is compassion, pain done already, no
   more suffering. It is a gift I pray for, if worthy, if
   God decides… I pray to God for safety, for good
   old age, enough money, clean bed, food, no pain.
   I ask not to be burden on my family, no burden
   on family, please. I ask for cure. Is possible, can,
   if God decides.

2 I think my Grandmother's still hoping for a cure.
   From Jesus, not the medical profession, she's
   given up on them. They say I'm doing great.
   *'He's broken lah! So suay, come out already need
   medicine. He feels very pain what.'*
   Cousin Nish says Grandmother's selectively
   Deaf – only listens to what she wants to. She
   doesn't hear what the doctor says… I'm doing
   great. My friend wants me to be cured, and I go
   'bro', you're worse than my Grandmother. It's
   impossible. This is congenital, this is genetic,

this is it, man, until the wooden overcoat, the
sky burial, until I go up in flames' and he goes
'everything is possible.' And that may be what
others want, fine – whatever gets you through the
night, you know? – but me? Respect, but I don't
want to be any other way. This is me. I'm not
in pain – well, nothing I can't handle – I don't
'suffer from' my condition. No, man, it's just who
I am, what I know, it's not a problem. If there is a
problem, it's not there. Some people are fine how
they are, you know?

Welsh variation:

I think my Grandmother's still hoping for a cure,
from Jesus, not the medical profession, she's given
up on them. She doesn't believe that I'm alright.
'*Duw, duw, duw. Ond dy'w o ddim yn iawn. Mae fo
'di torri – mae angen trwsio'r peth.' (Translates.)*
'But he's broken – he needs fixing, poor dab.'
I've decided she's selectively Deaf – only listens
to what she wants and she doesn't hear me. She
wants me to be cured, *i gwella,* and I go 'Nan, it's
impossible – *amhosib.* This is congenital, this is
genetic, this is it until the wooden overcoat, the
sky burial, until I go up in flames.'
And she goes: 'Everything is possible, *bach.*'

There's always someone wanting you to be different from how you are. If it's not being cured, it's 'embracing your identity as a disabled person.' I don't think like that – there's no 'dis' in my ability… And as to getting 'better' – I can't get 'better' when I'm already the best I'll ever be.

3   When my illness happened, many came to help and prayed with me – Christians, Taoists, Catholics. Buddhist friends took me to chant, to plead with the Goddess of Mercy. That didn't work. So my friends they brought me to the Muslim god, many Indian gods, Chinese god, Christian god… so many temples, so many churches, very Singapore, very *rojak – you char kway, tau pok* – so many flavours, many tastes, like a spiritual food court. So it is a church, then it is a mosque, then it is temple and still no cure and my friends wonder do I have doubt, or a bad heart? They try so hard, they pray so strong, yet nothing happens. They think it is me. 'Or maybe,' I say, 'maybe all of these gods want me to stay this way for a purpose.'

4   And people will suddenly do it, even strangers on the street, without introduction, without permission – they will start praying over me, or

chanting, or speaking in tongues and I know they mean well, but – really? Without asking first? Imagine if one of these uninvited faith healers laid their hands on you and you were changed – 'healed' – but you go 'I liked how I was. This is what I know… Now I have to start all over again.' You want to 'cure' me? Of what? My identity, my politics, my language, who I am? It's society that needs to be healed, made whole, not me. I don't want their prayers, I don't want their healing. I am happy as I am. Leave us signing, walking with our canes, rolling on our wheels, strutting with our crutches.

Is it their judgement that needs to be cured?

AND SUDDENLY I DISAPPEAR 2

For Kirstie Davis

And suddenly I disappear. My flesh dissolves and
I'm nowhere – suddenly not here – a blink and I
vanish – erased by your not looking, your I-see-
you-but-I-don't-see-you eyes. I'm gone, removed
in an instant, erased, deleted like a wrong answer,
struck through like a bad sum and I'm not there,
I've been rubbed out, wiped away, expunged,
reduced to naught. Nothing. Zero. Absence. Nil.
Zip.
Zilch.
Zero.
Naught.
Nada.
Nix.
Null.
Nil.
Nothing.
None.
Nowt.
Nought.
Nothing.

ANOMALY

It's about control. I know what is expected, what
is tolerated, what needs to be masked, what needs
to be on display. And when in public, I need to
be perfect: hair, clothes – I am playing a role.
I work hard at my invisibility, at my sustaining
a protective screen that is interpreted by those
around me as normality.

Alone, it is different.

Alone, I can relax.

In public, my mind needs to control, it needs to
keep watch, it needs to keep me in line otherwise
I'll throw scissors or act impulsively. I am an
anomaly, just like my country, this extraordinary
land that has achieved so much in such a short
time, but which now craves conformity. It can take
my being a perfectionist, it can take my success
and efficiency, it can take my ruthlessness so
long as that is part of my business strategy rather
than a quirk of my brain. I will do anything to
succeed, to obtain what my brain decides is next
– and I don't know if that's part of my condition,
or something I have been taught and have had
ingrained in me, a condition we all have. All of us
who are successful and wealthy, that is.

We have a choice, people like me. We could yield to our impulses, take personal or illegal risks – or use the same desire for that adrenaline rush but do it legitimately, do well in business, be manipulative and do anything short of murder – everything else is acceptable – except in business, we don't call it manipulative. We call it strategy; being articulate, passionate, persuasive. Effective. I'm the youngest and most successful salesperson in my team. I worked on myself to turn my disadvantage to advantage. I'm lauded as a great businessperson, as the employee of the year, as the person whose tactics and habits are exemplary and to be copied by others who also long for success and money... Would they see me the same way, aspire to be me if they knew all this was because of the mechanics of my brain? I'm a psychological Machiavellian. I ooze charm. I bring influence where my glance lands. I can make people love me, follow me, believe me, promote me.

But I can't do this in relationships, like I do in business deals. I become so focused on the endgame, I miss the game – the being here now, that human touch.

I'm lonely.

I can be brutal. I can use language like the finest surgeon's scalpel and cut through to the bone. But largely I choose not to destroy. I'm creative, good for other's self-esteem – I can quickly assess what colleagues need, how to problem-solve, fix, progress, and they go away feeling good about themselves. They ask how they can be more like me, but I cannot voice my formula, for it relies on a fault and so remains secret. And I have many dependants, many employees relying on me, so I lie, I keep the invisible invisible, even though it is the thing that makes me a success. I stigmatise my stigmatised self. I help hide and disempower myself for the sake of my dependants and a continued status quo, for to be open as to who I really am would risk failure and abandonment. Difference is tolerable when it fits established plans, ways and rules.

Can I risk revealing myself? Would I be embraced or feared, accepted or shunned?

I am an anomaly.

Before, when we were nation-building, anomalies were good.

BROKEN HANDLE

Her father said:
一个手柄已经坏了的勺子, 有什么用呢?
What use is a ladle with a broken handle?
She thought of all the things she had that weren't
perfect:
The dress with the crooked hem that made her
feel like a million dollars.
The old wooden table, scarred with use.
The vintage brooch bought in a junk shop on
holiday in Europe.
The children's drawings from school, stuck on the
fridge door.
Her aunt's engagement ring, missing the diamonds.
The moth-eaten shawl.
The worn bone handled knife.
The shelf propped up with books.
The watch that no longer keeps time
And she remembered:

                         the delight in the jagged
edge of the dropped cup, where the thin china
might split her lip, or not.

                         her favourite toy, battered
with love, falling apart from being held too close,
too tight.

                       the wonky wheel on the
tricycle which made her veer off the path in
exhilarating ways.
Who wants to be uniform?
She wants to be more than the regular factory
shop floor model, the conveyor belt of
conventional beauty.
She likes what's thought incomplete, odd, for
it is not incomplete or odd to itself – that is its
substance, its being. It is full in its form – whole –
not defunct.
Damaged goods get thrown away or sold at a
lesser price, his father said. But in the bargain
basement, what treasures you can find.
The cracked pot gets shoved into the back of
the cupboard, her grandmother said. It is kept
apart, not suitable for company, just for holding
leftovers or the dog's slops, where it could be
kicked across the floor and not matter if it breaks.
I am all and none of these things.
I am the fly in the amber
the grit that makes the pearl
the crack that lets in the dawn.

I will not be wiped away.
I am your daughter.
I am your son.
I am not ash, mere bone.
I am not bound to the earth.

I am a river. A river that does not stop.
It finds its way. It carves through stone, through rock.
It always finds a way to flow on.
成为水, 成为河[13]
Be a river that doesn't stop.

This is how we will be,
Unstoppable. Fluid. Powerful.
Independent, following our own route,
our own way.

For suddenly, I start to appear
I start to appear
I start to appear…

---

13 Be a river, be like water.

THE ENVY OF THE WORLD

We used to be the envy of the world: the best practice others aspired to. Oh well, everything changes. Two steps forward, ten steps back.

I like to keep myself nice. It's hard in a care home, you get all sorts, but I do my best to keep us a happy crew. It's nice to be nice and it doesn't cost anything to have manners, but could cost you a lot more in the long run if someone gets the hump. Leave you in the bath and everything, water cooling. A carer did that the other day – Joe – helped me in over the high sides, passed me the Imperial Leather and then plain forgot about me. His hearing's not the best and once he had me in the tub he got distracted when Bill – one of the other residents – fell down the stairs. Again. We keep saying they should put a child's gate on those stairs as Bill will keep trying to roll down them like he's at the winter Olympics, but they won't listen. '*You need to get a proper lift, not that chair thing that breaks down all the time,*' he yells when they expect him to go up and down on this b.t.m. Maintenance staff for Stenna chairlifts are apparently at a premium. '*I was made sell my house to pay for my care here, so the least you could do is protect my dignity.*'

Well, with all that palaver and an incident form to fill in, Joe clean forgot about me, and then he couldn't hear me yelling. Not that he'd admit that. He'd prefer to be thought rude rather than one of us. It's like keeping difference between infantry and officer class. Keeps the hoi from the polloi, he thinks. Not good for morale. If we're all the same, who'd be helping who?

Baths. Dangerous things. I much prefer a shower. A wet room – that's what they have over in Ferndale Care Home – nothing to trip you up or clamber over and there's even a little flip-down chair if it all gets too much and you fancy a sit down.

Ferndale's class. But you don't always get what you pay for, that's what I've learned from being here. What they spend all that money on, I couldn't say, but it isn't the quality of the breakfast cereal, safety of the bathroom, or comfort of the beds. Mary says those walk-in whatnots and modulating air mattresses at Ferndale don't buy themselves. *'24 hour care and integrated nursing staff doesn't grow on trees,'* she tells me. *'Your pound goes further here, so long as you're not the fussy kind.'* And she says 'fussy' in such a way you can tell it's a bad thing. I just nod and say 'yes, nurse.' Not that she is. They are, over in

Ferndale, trained and everything, but Mary's just
for wiping spills and helping you to the toilet. I
call her 'nurse' to make her feel better.

'I wanted to leave that house to my kids,' Bill says
several times over dinner, still going on about it,
*'not that I had a say in it. I'd've preferred a one way
trip to Switzerland rather than coming here.'*
Always fancied Austria, myself.

*

People are always complaining about this...*home's*
not the right word – this *place*. It has its moments.
I like not having to crawl everywhere, as I used
to in my old flat. It was social housing, narrow
doorways on the top floor of an inaccessible
tower block, which was impossible the days I
needed to use my wheelchair. That's what the
council didn't understand – the randomness of
how my body works; it isn't stable, some days
are better than others. Some days I can manage
on my feet, and others it's wheels all the way, but
there isn't a box to tick for that on the forms they
use to assess our needs and what we're entitled to.
I used to get my friend Fran to come round and
help me wash after my disability allowance was
cut – carers halved to fifteen minutes twice a day,
so there was no time for them to help me shower,

just a flick round with a wet wipe, a cup of tea and sandwich as they headed out of the door, late for their next appointment.

How we laughed. It was hysterical, trying to get me and Fran into the tiny bathroom at the same time, with me hanging over the bath as she tried to wash my hair – like an obstacle course – but that ended once her subsidised transport was stopped because of money-saving cutbacks. *'We want a country of strivers, not skivers'* the government says, which makes Fran angry, as she used to be a tax payer and independent until they withdrew her transport, so she had to stop work because there isn't a route to her job via accessible public transport, and taxis are too expensive. So there she is, like Rapunzel back in the tower, locked into her flat like I was – these islands of isolation, like living in a lighthouse in the middle of a wild sea, with no boat. So at least there's some company here, even if it's not by choice.

I've had to loosen up about things, like privacy, and get used to men like Joe stripping me, bathing me, and seeing me naked. That took some getting used to. It's humiliating having a young man handle your body when only my husband saw me naked before. They try to make a joke about it, but when time's an issue – which it always is – Joe's slap-dash handling makes me feel like a lump of meat being rolled and trussed up for the oven. He doesn't mean to be rough, but his hands are hard. Still, it's good to feel clean, much better than having to last the day in the same clothes until your carer comes. I've always hated the word 'soiled'. And then the carers used to get cross about how I tried to stretch out my incontinence pads. Once the council stopped providing them for free, I couldn't afford them as well as food.

'I thought this was England,' Fran said on our weekly catch-up on the phone, *'not a third world country.'*

How we laughed.

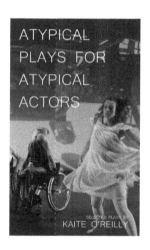